Crescent Color Guide to
Ponies

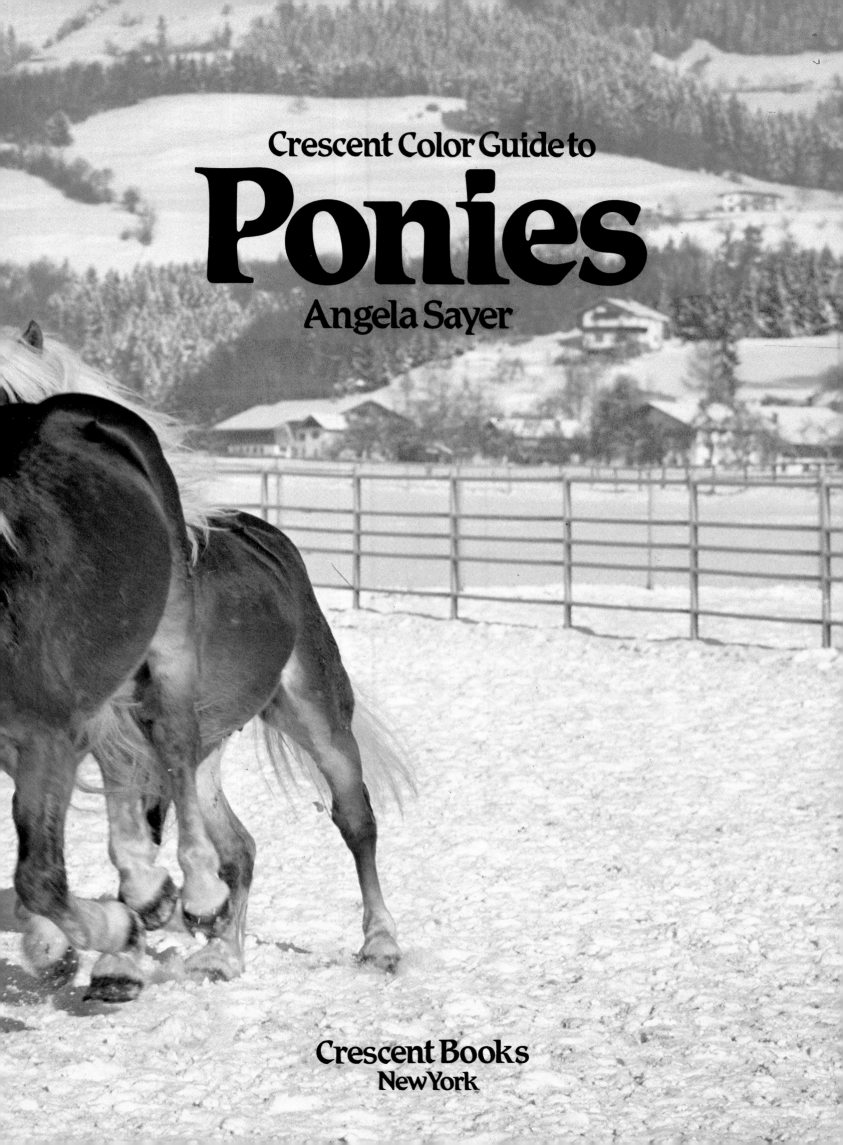

Crescent Color Guide to
Ponies
Angela Sayer

Crescent Books
New York

Photography by Angela Sayer
(Tony Stone Associates: pages 7, 8, 13, 17, 27, 49, 51, 73, 79.
Ardea London Ltd: page 39. Ardea London Ltd – John
Daniels: pages 19, 24. Ardea London Ltd – Richard Waller:
page 20 bottom. Ardea London Ltd – Jean-Paul Ferrero:
page 42. Bruce Coleman Ltd – Hans Reinhard: pages 18, 55,
56. Bruce Coleman – Jane Burton: pages 20 top, 76 right.
Equestrian (Photographic Services) Ltd: pages 40, 47. Pictor
International: pages 57, 59, 65)

Copyright © The Hamlyn Publishing Group Limited MCMLXXXI

First English edition published by
The Hamlyn Publishing Group Limited
London · New York · Sydney · Toronto
Astronaut House, Feltham, Middlesex, England

Library of Congress Catalog Card Number:
ISBN 0-517-34185-9

This edition is published by Crescent Books,
a division of Crown Publishers, Inc.
a b c d e f g h

Printed in Italy

Contents

What is a Pony?

The term PONY is used to describe small varieties of the horse family, and should not be used to describe a young horse, which is properly known as a *foal*. Both horses and ponies give birth to foals, a male foal being called a *colt*, and a female, a *filly*. Fillies grow up to become *mares* at four years of age, while colts mature as *stallions* unless castrated at an early age so that they grow on to become more manageable and easily trained *geldings*. Although all ponies are of the same basic construction, some have fine bones and a light conformation and are therefore suitable as children's riding ponies, while others are more robust and sturdy, ideal for driving and other draught work.

A good pony has a well-proportioned body, with powerful shoulders and hindquarters for speed and performance. The strong muscular neck supports a long head equipped with a modified jaw which contains two sets of teeth. The front set is designed to tear grasses and herbs which are then passed to the rear set of cheek teeth where the material is methodically ground down into an easily digestible state before being swallowed. The teeth undergo regular and distinct changes throughout the pony's life, and a knowledge of this characteristic allows the animal's age to be determined by checking its dentition pattern.

As in most herbivorous animals, the eyes of the pony are set wide apart on either side of its head, allowing it almost all-round vision as a natural defence. The nostrils are flexible with the ability to flare wide open, allowing the pony to catch the merest whiff of any warning scent and also facilitating the intake of extra oxygen to its lungs when galloping at full speed. The pony's ears are also very flexible, making it possible for it to catch and pinpoint the direction of the slightest unusual sound. These mobile ears may be used as a barometer of your pony's feelings, for when they are held back the animal is feeling bored or bad-tempered and, if they are laid back flat to the head, the pony is warning that it might well bite or kick.

The Spring Buck is a six-month-old foal showing great promise in his conformation, presence and style.

Some ponies, like this attractive chestnut, make dual-purpose pets, suitable for both riding and driving.

The pony usually has long strong legs with hooves of hard, insensitive horn which is constantly renewing itself. The wide round sole with its central rubbery and triangular frog gives the pony safe footing on rough or slippery ground. There are strange horny lumps, known as *chestnuts*, on the insides of the pony's four legs, and long coarse hairs grow from the ridge along the top of its neck to form a mane, while similar long hairs grow from the short, bony tail. Some ponies have long soft hair growing from their heels, which helps to protect them in cold wet weather.

Ponies are thought to have originated centuries ago in Central Asia and gradually migrated westwards to Europe, east to China and Mongolia and south to Egypt, Persia and India. As small herds settled in suitable areas along these main routes, natural selection and the demands of the individual environments caused the gradual diversification that eventually produced the types, colours and breeds that we know today.

In the colder northern areas, ponies needed to develop the ability to grow thick winter coats in order to survive, while in the warmer climes to the south, ponies with thin skins and fine coats eventually evolved, and in the tropical areas of the world, ponies developed powers of strength and endurance that belied their often puny appearance. Wherever a pony population found itself a suitable niche, it settled, multiplied and prospered.

This pretty little pony is just the right size to make a perfect pet for a small child.

These two youngsters are play-fighting, practising the behaviour patterns of adult members of their herd.

Eventually, man intervened in nature's affairs and, by controlling matings, was able to produce specific breeds and types of pony for special purposes. Desirable characteristics were strengthened and unwanted traits gradually bred out until many countries, and sometimes regions within countries, developed their own recognizable pony breeds. From being merely a source of meat hunted by early man, the pony proved its worth first as a pack animal, then in agricultural draught work, and eventually as a war machine, drawing chariots and carrying armed warriors.

In the wild state, ponies may start breeding at two years of age given an adequate supply of food and water, and mares generally produce a foal each spring after a gestation period of about 340 days. The mare produces rich milk, suckling its baby for some months even after it is able to graze efficiently, and it is common in wild herds to see mares closely accompanied by their yearlings as well as their current foals. The wild pony stallions fight for superiority and for the privilege of serving the mares in each small group, and colts reaching maturity are usually driven off to form small bachelor herds on their own. In this way only the fittest and the most suitable bloodlines are carried forward, following successful patterns of development of the horse family through the millions of years of its evolution.

Above: Isolation of gene pools and the selective breeding practices of man helped to produce specific types and breeds like the Haflinger.

Left: Mongolian Wild Horse mares and foals graze peacefully in the protection of the pastures in San Diego's Wild Life Park.

Much has been learned of the ancestors of today's ponies from a study of the MONGOLIAN WILD HORSE (*Equus przevalskii przevalskii*) or POLJAKOFF, discovered by a Russian explorer in 1881. The wild herds were found in the remote Kobdo regions of Mongolia, and their discovery caused great excitement when it was realized that here were some animals that had remained virtually unchanged in appearance since the last great Ice Age. Eventually some foals were caught, and there are now several successful breeding herds of Poljakoff in captivity. The Mongolian Wild Horse stands between 12 and 14 hands, and is dun in colour although the shade may range from the palest cream-dun to the deepest golden-dun. The legs are dark and sometimes have zebra markings, and the spine sports a dark dorsal stripe. The tail of the Poljakoff is rather thinly furnished with coarse dark hair, and the short thick mane forms an erect crest right along the neck. Some of the features of this interesting animal may still be found in our modern pony breeds.

Today the pony is found in many shapes, colours, patterns and sizes. Ponies are used for all aspects of riding – hacking, trekking, hunting, jumping, in competitions and as therapy for the disabled. They are used for driving and for working the land, and some are kept as pampered and cherished pets. People keep ponies for a wide variety of reasons: to some they are status symbols, to others they are a necessity of life, but all ponies need regular feeding, care and attention. Whether for riding, driving, breeding or just loving, there is a pony to suit every purpose, although finding this perfect pony sometimes takes time.

This pony has a thick mane and tail with lots of hair around its legs, helping to combat the wintry weather of its native home, Scotland's Isle of Skye.

Choosing a Pony

A FAMILY PONY

A pony suitable for family use may be of any shape or size, and need not be of any particular pedigree breed. It must however be fit, in good health and active, and sufficiently hardy to enable it to live outside in a field all year round. It must be strong enough to carry any member of the family that wishes to ride, and must be gentle enough to respond to the aids of the smallest children. The pony must have a kind and intelligent nature and must not have formed any really bad habits.

The family pony need not be very handsome, but its conformation should be good enough to ensure that all paces are performed smoothly and comfortably. If a pony has a short thick neck, its head may be carried too low, while a ewe-necked pony carries its head unnaturally high. Both these ponies would be awkward and ungainly at fast paces or when jumping. Straight shoulders in a pony produce a sharp stilted action at the trot and underdeveloped withers allow the saddle to slip too far forward. Conversely, weak sloping quarters or a long straight back both tend to encourage the saddle to slide too far back.

In choosing any pony, great attention must be paid to the conformation and condition of its legs and feet. The pony should stand squarely on all four legs and should be examined from the front and from behind to see that there are no deviations from vertical lines. A pony whose hocks turn inwards is called *cowhocked* while one whose hocks bend under the body is called *sickle-hocked*. A cowhocked pony has faulty paces, while one with sickle hocks may tend to go lame quite frequently. The hindlegs should be well shaped with strong, clean-cut hocks and well-developed second thighs, and the forelegs should have strong, muscular forearms and sharply defined knees with flat planes.

This magnificent New Forest stallion is a fine example of good conformation in the pony.

This is a good family pony, strong, sturdy and obviously possessed of a kind, even temperament.

A pony such as this one spends long hours working cattle, so it is important that he has a calm temperament and considerable stamina.

On all four legs, the lower bone is known as the *cannon* and should be short and strong. It joins the *pastern* by the *fetlock joint* which in turn joins the hard hoof at the *coronet* with a fringe of fine short hair. The formation of this structure – fetlock–pastern–hoof – is very important, acting as it does as a shock absorption system for the pony.

Unless you intend to breed from your pony, it will not matter very much whether it is a mare or a gelding. Stallions are not suitable for use as general riding ponies, although some well-behaved pony stallions are shown under saddle by quite young riders. A mare will come into breeding season at regular intervals, and if she is inclined to be temperamental at such times this could be a disadvantage. However, mares often seem to be more intelligent than geldings, and are sometimes found to be extremely affectionate towards their owners. A well-brought-up gelding rarely has problems of temperament and, if properly treated, may also be kind and affectionate.

When choosing a pony, one of the most important things to think about is its size. It must be tall and strong enough to carry you through all the riding activities that you expect to undertake, but if you want to enter riding classes, you must be sure that the pony is of the correct height for those classes. If you are small and slight, you must make sure that the pony is not too strong or perhaps too wide for your comfort. And in these days of congested, busy roads, it is essential to buy a pony that is well behaved and safe in traffic.

Unless you are very knowledgeable, you should take along an expert when you go to try out a potential pony, for it is important to select the animal for the right reasons, as well as ensuring that it is sound and quite suitable, since buying a pony is a big step and not one to be undertaken lightly. The best way to acquire a pony is by buying from friends or neighbours who have an outgrown family pet; you will then know all about the animal's virtues as well as its faults, and you will probably also be able to buy its own comfortable saddle and bridle. You may decide to scour the advertisements in horse and pony magazines or in the newspaper, to discover probable purchases. You need to write down your basic requirements before you start to search – height, type and ability, age and preferred colours – then make a short list of possible purchases.

Above: This bright chestnut foal has a distinctive white facial marking known as a 'blaze'.

Left: This young Palomino is being shown in-hand and is learning to stand up correctly in order to show himself off to prospective purchasers.

COLOURS AND MARKINGS

The range of colours of ponies is very large, enough to suit every taste, and there are many old rhymes and superstitions concerning their colours and markings. There is no basis of truth behind these, except perhaps the one that states 'a good horse is never a bad colour'. The term BLACK is self-explanatory, although true black ponies are fairly rare, and some dark brown ponies may appear to be black. The test for a genuine black is to examine the fine short hairs on the muzzle which are an indication of the true colour. BROWN appears in several shades, and is considered to be a very smart colour for show ponies. Brown ponies often have black legs, manes and tails and such animals are said to have black *points*. BAY is a very bright colour which varies from a rich pale brown colour to a deep mahogany hue. It is also considered to be a good colour for show stock and many bays also have black points.

The term GREY is used to describe ponies which may vary in colour from almost pure white to dark steel-grey. Some have dappled markings, others may be *flea-bitten greys* with dark flecks in the coat. Some grey ponies are born almost black and lighten as they mature, reaching their true colour at about four years of age or more. Other greys may lighten until they are pure white in old age. There are very few truly white ponies and most of these prove to be *albino*, with unpigmented skin and very light eyes. Most grey ponies have very dark and lustrous eyes, and the mane and tail are generally formed from black-and-white intermingled hairs.

CHESTNUT is a variable shade ranging from the palest golden-brown to the darkest liver colour. Few ponies are totally chestnut as most have white markings on the legs and face. Their manes and tails may be of a matching chestnut, palely flaxen or very dark.

DUN is the colour of the prehistoric pony, but has survived until the present day. It obviously evolved to match the ancient animal's dusty, sandy plains environment. Dun ponies generally also retain the ancient eel-stripe of black hairs along the spine; they often have black points and occasionally have pale beige muzzles. The dun colour is extremely variable, and some shades are rare but very beautiful.

CREAM ponies are paler than dun, and quite rare, and a true cream should have a silver mane and tail. When white hairs are present flecked throughout a pony's coat, the resulting effect is called ROAN, and there are *strawberry-roan*, *blue-roan* and *red-roan* ponies. SORREL is similar to roan but is of intermingled red and black hairs without any white.

COLOURED ponies are those which are *piebald*, *skewbald* or *odd-coloured*. They are favoured by gipsies and horse-traders throughout the world and were often revered by the North American Indian tribes in earlier years. The piebald is a white pony with irregular patches of dense black. The skewbald is white with patches of either brown, bay or chestnut, while odd-coloured ponies are white with patches of two or more colours.

A pony may have WHITE MARKINGS on the head or legs and these have special names, used when describing the animal in advertisements or on registration documents. A *star* is the name for any white mark on the pony's forehead, while a *stripe* is a narrow white stripe running down the face. If the stripe extends beyond the front of the nasal bones, it is called a *blaze*, but if it also covers the forehead, the muzzle or the cheeks the pony is called *white-faced*. Small, random white facial marks, except on the forehead, are called *snips*.

White markings on the legs have been known as *socks* and *stockings* for many years, but for registration purposes they have to be described very accurately, such as 'white fetlock'. Chestnut ponies with four white legs and a white stripe or blaze are very showy and belie the old rhyme:

> Four white legs – keep him not a day,
> Three white legs – send him far away,
> Two white legs – give him to your friend, but
> One white leg – keep him to the end.

PEDIGREE POINTS

The majority of ponies suitable for general riding purposes are crossbred animals, and come in every conceivable combination of shape, size, colour and markings. Some show the influence of Thoroughbred or Arabian bloodlines;

This skewbald is strikingly marked, though of poor conformation with weak quarters, straight shoulders and a ewe-neck.

others are the result of crossing two or more native breeds. It is sometimes preferable, however, to buy a pedigree pony for, by choosing a suitable breed, you may be able to ride it under saddle in special show classes and, if it is a mare, perhaps breed from her when she is outgrown or reaches retirement age.

When various islands of the world were becoming populated, small breeds of horse were often trans-shipped along with other livestock, to be used in haulage work and the development of human settlements. As the years passed, such ponies bred and eventually, due to the confines of an island habitat, developed into unique standardized breeds. Islanders became proud of their native ponies and took care to prevent any infusion of undesirable blood from imported stock.

The British Isles, in particular, are well endowed with pony breeds for its climate and geology provide ideal conditions for the natural rearing of hardy animals, known and loved around the world. The most ancient of the British breeds is the EXMOOR PONY, said to be the descendant of the British Wild Horse and a truly indigenous animal preserved in its aboriginal state to the present time. During the Ice Ages, Exmoor was one of the few parts of the British Isles not covered by ice, and so the ancient ponies were able to survive. A finely built pony of about 12·2 hands high, the Exmoor can carry extraordinary weights for its size, and is often used for foxhunting by farmers on its native moorlands. The Exmoor always has a characteristic 'mealy' muzzle, the colour of oatmeal whatever its body colour, which may be bay, brown or dun. Its coat is harsh, dull and springy in the winter, close, smooth and gleaming in the summer, and foals have double, weatherproof coats for protection, consisting of thick wool-like undercoats and top coats of long harsh hair.

Below: Norwegian Fjord Ponies have the 'mealy' muzzle and dark dorsal stripe found in the Mongolian Wild Horse. Their body colour is known as dun.

Right: An Exmoor mare and foal, strong and very hardy, and both with typical 'mealy' muzzles.

A five-day-old
Dartmoor Pony foal
sleeps peacefully
against its mother.

Exmoor ponies can be strong-willed youngsters and need time and
patience at breaking-in. They are adept at escaping from any enclosure and
so need strong well-made fences and gates in their paddocks. Many horse
breeders have used Exmoor stock in their foundation matings from which
have been developed really strong and sensible hunters and show jumpers. In
fact, one winner of the famous Grand National steeplechase had its pedigree
traced back to an Exmoor ancestor. This pony makes an ideal mount for
young children, being narrow and sure-footed, and is also excellent in
harness.

This New Forest
Pony foal is
determined not to let
its mother doze in
peace.

Another type of pony evolved in Dartmoor, a bleak and forbidding area of moorland in the extreme south-west of England. The area's rocky slopes and gullies, often swept by fierce gales, ensured that only the fittest ponies survived and the mineral-enriched herbage of the moor endowed them with strong bones and tough, well-shaped hooves. The DARTMOOR was originally used as a pit pony and for packing loads over rough country but, unlike the Exmoor, it had regular infusions of Thoroughbred, Hackney and Arabian blood through the centuries. In recent years, steps have been taken to standardize this pony and regulate breeding practices. Up to 12·2 hands in height and allowed in any colour, except piebald and skewbald, today's Dartmoor is a very pretty pony with a beautiful head, small alert ears and a fine muzzle. Its shoulders, quarters and back are strong, and these qualities, combined with a kind and generous nature, make it an ideal child's pony for riding in show classes.

In the south of England, the vast expanses of the New Forest provide grazing for about 3,000 ponies on common land. The NEW FOREST PONY is generally bay or brown but several other recognized pony colours are seen, and it may be up to 14·2 hands high. The typical specimen has a rather large head on a short strong neck, good shoulders and a deep girth with plenty of heart room. The quarters are rather narrow and sloping, and the legs are strong with good bone and hard feet. An excellent family pony, the 'Forester' is generally traffic-proof and a very good jumper, safe and reliable at all times.

Groups of New Forest ponies inhabit specific areas, known as 'haunts', and each adult has its tail distinctively marked to show that its owner has paid the annual fee for grazing in the forest. Each autumn the annual roundup takes place when all the young stock is gathered in for identification and tail-marking or for sale in the auction ring. Various stallions have been allowed to breed with the forest mares over the years, resulting in a strong versatile breed with a Thoroughbred presence combined with an inherent toughness.

In the north of England, the Pennine Mountains form a rocky ridge which divided an ancient pony herd into two groups which eventually diversified to develop into two distinct, but still obviously closely related, breeds. To the east of the range, the magnificent DALES PONY came into being, while on the western side the great FELL PONY was born.

During the nineteenth century, Dales ponies were used to carry lead from the mines of Northumberland and Durham to the docks. The great loads weighing over 220 pounds (100 kg) were slung in twin panniers on either side of the ponies' backs, and they were expected to cover about 240 miles (380 km) each week. To this day the worn pathways remain, cut deep into the rocky terrain by the patiently plodding hooves.

The Dales pony can be up to 14·2 hands high and is heavily built with a neat head and small, well-placed ears. The back is fairly short and the shoulders and quarters well-developed and very strong. The legs have good bone and are well-muscled, while the hooves are typically hard and well shaped, fringed on the heels by fine and silky hair. The Dales is very useful for agricultural work especially in hilly areas unsuitable for tractors. It makes a sturdy riding pony too, ideal for family use and in the hunting field, where its willing but placid nature gives confidence to the nervous novice. Being also very good in harness, strong and quiet in traffic, and economical to feed, the Dales is perhaps the perfect ride-and-drive pony, honest, hardy and handsome.

Like the Dales, the Fell pony was also used to carry lead from the mines to the Tyneside docks. In droves of twenty, led by a man on horseback, the sturdy animals carried their heavily laden panniers at a steady walk over the rocky roads. During the same period, farmers owning Fells organized trotting races, and some of the ponies were found to be capable of trotting at great speed. Later it became fashionable to cross Fell ponies with Thoroughbreds to produce fine hunters and show-jumping horses – the world-famous eventer, Merely-a-Monarch, was the grandson of a Fell mare.

The pure-bred Fell pony is used for hunting, trekking, shepherding and long-distance riding as well as being an ideal driving pony. Up to 14 hands in height, it is generally black although brown, bay and grey coat colour is also allowed. The pony has a small, well-chiselled head with a broad forehead, large nostrils and bright, intelligent eyes. The neck is moderately long and set into very strong and sloping shoulders, and the short muscular back meets square, sturdy quarters with a well-set tail. Very sturdy legs end in round feet formed of a characteristic hard blue horn, and there is plenty of fine silky hair at the heels. The action of the Fell is well balanced and rather showy, and the pony has great powers of endurance. These attributes, combined with a kind, placid temperament, make the Fell an ideal all-round family pony.

Another heavy breed of pony is the magnificent HIGHLAND which originated in the Western Isles and the Outer Hebrides and on the mainland of Scotland. From fossil remains it is claimed that this breed is directly descended from an old race of horses that existed before the last great Ice Age. There are two distinct types of Highland, the smaller pure-bred being from 13 to 14 hands high, and the larger Garron, 14 to 14·2 hands high. For generations this pony was used for pack purposes, in agriculture and in the deer forests, carrying out the weighty carcasses of culled stags. Perhaps the most neglected of all the British native pony breeds, the Highland has recently enjoyed a new wave of popularity.

Below: Highland Ponies are noted for their rare colours. This magnificent stallion is a silver-dun.

Right: The smaller type of Highland Pony is very hardy and makes an excellent jumper with a good, even temperament.

Shetland Ponies have been existing in their native islands for more than 2,000 years.

The Highland is very comfortable to ride, and has immense strength for its size which, combined with its intelligent appraisal of most situations, makes it an ideal hunting pony. The smaller type of Highland has a neat head with small pricked ears and large expressive eyes, often of a golden-hazel colour. The body and legs are sturdy and stocky, and the mane and tail are thick and luxurious, the heels feathered with a little silky hair. They make excellent jumping ponies and have the special sort of temperament that makes them very responsive to kind, firm treatment and training.

The larger type of Highland is a magnificent pony with an abundant mane and tail and feathered heels. In this breed, beautifully coloured ponies are often produced, for in addition to the usual blacks and browns there are beautiful bays and lovely shades of grey and cream. Sometimes a liver chestnut may appear with a silver mane and tail, and there is a whole range of dun colours: blue-dun, silver-dun, mouse-dun and many other colours. The yellow-dun is said to be the colour of the original animal, reverting back through the generations to its wild ancestry and, like most duns, often showing a black dorsal line, an eel-stripe. With dark points, and a rather mealy effect on the muzzle, its eel-stripe and faint zebra marking on the legs, a good yellow-dun Highland is a distinctive and very beautiful pony, echoing its origins.

Just as the largest of the British ponies originated in Scotland, so did the smallest – the diminutive SHETLAND, a native of Orkney and the Shetland Islands where it has existed for 2,000 years. Its small size is thought to have been produced by generations of existence in a harsh, inhospitable environment. But despite its tiny size, the Shetland has personality plus and should never be underestimated; it is quick to learn both good and bad habits and, if properly treated, makes a perfect pet.

23

The pedigree Shetland may be of any colour and is unique in being measured only in inches, rather than in hands. Registered stock must not exceed 40 inches at three years of age and 42 inches at four years and over. The head of the Shetland is small and well-shaped, broad between the dark, intelligent eyes and with small ears. The neck is strong and has a particularly well-developed crest, especially in the stallion. The shoulders are oblique and the body short and deep with strong quarters. The shortish legs are well-made with good bone and the feet should be open – round – and very tough. The profuse mane and tail set off the little pony's looks to perfection.

In the islands of its birth, the Shetland often had to exist on seaweed and lichen when the winter snows covered the scant pasture. It was used as a pack pony for carrying all manner of loads including panniers of seaweed used for fertilizing the crofters' fields. Later the Shetland, sometimes crossed with other small breeds, was used to produce the hundreds of ponies needed for work below ground in the coal-mines of Britain during the Industrial Revolution. Today, Shetland ponies are used for driving and for small children to ride. They are also to be seen performing clever tricks in the circuses of the world, as mascots leading regimental parades and acting as companions to larger horses and ponies.

The thick mane of the Shetland Pony gives protection against the harsh environment of the islands.

24

A Connemara stallion in his in-hand showing bridle, waiting for the judges.

Overleaf: This Welsh Mountain Pony foal is losing its dark baby coat, and will soon turn grey, just like its mother.

On the western side of Ireland exists an open, windswept region known as the Connemara, and here, on the lush mineral-enriched pastures, evolved the beautiful pony which bears the same name. Though its origins are obscure it has been said that the ancestors of the CONNEMARA PONY were small horses that swam ashore from shipwrecked vessels which then mated with the indigenous Celtic ponies. In the nineteenth century Arabian and Welsh stallions were introduced to the herds and their influence is clearly seen in the beautiful heads of the Connemara ponies of today.

The Connemara pony stands between 13 to 14 hands high and is often grey in colour, although black, brown, bay and dun are also permitted, and occasionally roan and chestnut animals are produced. Beautifully proportioned and possessed of a kind and intelligent nature, it makes an ideal riding pony with good jumping potential. Crossed with Thoroughbred stock, Connemara mares have produced some outstanding and famous offspring which have won top-class dressage and eventing competitions.

Also showing the results of infusions of Arabian blood is the delightful little WELSH MOUNTAIN PONY which has a history that can be traced back to the days of Julius Caesar's occupation of Britain. The great emperor arranged for the breeding of ponies under controlled conditions in studs along the shores of Lake Bala in North Wales. Welsh ponies and cobs are divided into four distinct sections, numbered 'A', 'B', 'C' and 'D'. The Mountain Pony Section 'A' is the smallest in the series and must not measure more than 12 hands high, and may be of any recognized equine colour except piebald or skewbald. Beautifully proportioned, this pony has a small, often dished head (inherited from its Arabian forebears), bold dark eyes and sharply pricked ears. The shoulders should be long and sloping, and the short back and good quarters ensure a comfortable ride. The pony's swift action is produced by

very large, flat hocks and well-developed knees. The Welsh Mountain pony has a character and temperament to match its good looks, and makes a superb first pony for any child, as well as going well in harness.

The WELSH PONY Section B is slightly larger, being up to 13·2 hands in height, and is perhaps the perfect pony for children to ride in show and performance classes. Also up to 13·2 hands high but up to a little more weight, is the WELSH PONY OF COB-TYPE Section 'C', and over 13·2 hands high is the famous WELSH COB Section 'D'. Ponies from Sections 'C' and 'D' must be sturdy, strong and active, and may be of any colour except piebald or skewbald. The head must be of refined pony type, and a coarse head or a Roman nose are considered faults. The eyes should be bold and prominent, and the ears small and neat. The body of the cob is deep with strong sloping shoulders and lengthy hindquarters, with legs that are very strong and muscular and heels which have soft silky feathering.

The action of the Section 'C' and 'D' animals is showy, especially at the trot; they are comfortable to ride and able to give a good account of themselves during a day's hunting.

Below: A Welsh Pony, Section 'B', makes a perfect show pony for an ambitious child.

Right: This Lundy Island Pony mare shares the windswept plateau with the rest of the herd and many equally hardy sheep.

The Camargue Pony often has to wander far and wide to find grazing and enjoys nibbling marsh plants and reeds.

It is interesting to trace the development of the intermediate types from the crossing of the fairylike Mountain Pony with the massive Welsh Cob. The small variety is most suitable for riding and drawing small vehicles, while the heavier Section 'C' animal makes a superb ride-and-drive pony for any member of the family. It is probably true to say that, whatever your requirements in a pony, you should be able to find them among the varied and versatile Welsh.

Exmoor and Connemara stallions were used in the establishment of a small breeding herd of ponies on Lundy, a small granite island 23 miles (40 km) off England's Devonshire coast. A natural home for many large seabirds, including puffins and gannets, the island is topped by a flat, windswept plateau from which steep, sea-carved cliffs descend to the sea. The original mares were of New Forest stock, shipped to the island in 1929, but with selective breeding practices, a distinct type has emerged that is recognized in its own right. Dun in colour, the LUNDY PONY stands about 13·2 hands high, and the sometimes harsh environment in which it is born ensures that it is strong and hardy. The Lundy makes an excellent competitive pony for children, being receptive to kind schooling, and is energetic, agile and a very good jumper.

Another product of an often inhospitable habitat is the CAMARGUE PONY which lives in the salt marshes of the Rhone Valley in southern France. They are used in herding the great black fighting bulls of the region, being ridden hard and fast over the difficult terrain by the local cowboys, and some are kept to carry tourists through the marshlands to view the area's famous flamingos and other wading birds. About 14·2 hands high, the Camargue pony is generally grey in colour, the foals being born very dark grey, almost black, and gradually turning paler as they mature. In winter, the working ponies are usually turned loose to find their own grazing, foraging among the reeds, often up to their bellies in water. On the Continent, the Camargue pony is sometimes acquired for private use and proves itself to be an admirable riding pony, needing very little food in relation to its work and having exceptional powers of endurance.

One of the rarest of all the pedigree ponies is the CASPIAN, which looks and moves like a miniature Arabian horse, and is believed to be the ancestor of the Arabian of today, as both Arabians and Caspians have unusual vaulted foreheads, very fine bone and remarkably dense horn in their hooves. The Caspian was thought to be extinct until an expedition, searching for small ponies suitable for teaching children to ride, found some of these attractive ponies on the shores of the Caspian Sea in Iran, where it was known as the MOULEKI or POUSEKI PONY. Specimens of the breed were purchased, being virtually rescued from lives of drudgery between the shafts of overloaded carts and under massive loaded panniers of firewood. Some were found in the rice fields, others on the high mountain slopes. Many were sick, beaten and bruised and all were suffering severely from parasitic infestations. The ponies were taken to Tehran where a small stud was established for the treatment and study of the animals. Later, breeding programmes were instituted and eventually stock was shipped to Bermuda, Britain and the United States.

The Caspian pony has emerged as a truly beautiful pony, 11 to 12 hands high with a short fine head, low flared nostrils and large, lustrous eyes. The ears are short and alert, and the graceful neck leads into well-defined withers. The back is fairly short and the quarters fine but strong with the flowing tail set high. The slim legs have fine bone and there is no sign of feathering on the fetlocks; the hooves are oval and so hard that the pony rarely needs shoeing. The action of the Caspian is smooth and comfortable, and its temperament is kind and gentle, making it the perfect breed for use as a first pony for a small or nervous child. Despite its small size, this pony has an impressive jumping ability and a great flair for work in harness, especially in pairs.

Klaus is a superb and famous leopard-spotted stallion, proud and elegant.

This tiny Caspian foal will grow into a miniature horse of only 11 or 12 hands high.

SPOTTED horses and ponies have been recorded since ancient times. They were known in China as Heavenly Horses and were first imported by Emperor Wu Ti around 100 B.C. Much prized by the ruling classes of those days, Emperor Hsuan T'sung is reputed to have had many spotted steeds among the 40,000 equines in his stables.

Rustan, a warrior of 400 B.C. always rode his spotted charger, Rakush, when he went into battle, and the indomitable pair were revered and feared as adversaries. It is said that all the spotted horses of Persia were directly descended from Rakush.

There have been many famous spotted horses in history, but perhaps best known today is the type known as the APPALOOSA, developed in the Palouse area of Idaho in the United States by the Nez Percé Indians, from stock introduced by the Spanish *conquistadores*. The spots of the Appaloosa may be felt by touch, as these stand in relief on the fine white coat. There are several different spotted patterns allowed in the show ring, including the *leopard spotted* which may have spots of any colour on a white or light background; the *blanket spotted* which has a white rump or back on which there are spots of any colour; and the *snowflake spotted* which has white spots on a foundation of any colour. Spotted ponies should be of good all-riding type, and often prove themselves to be good jumpers.

Above: *The Gemsbok*, a Palomino filly foal of ten weeks, showing the typical pale cream coat, and the golden colour just starting to show on the limbs.

Top: The Haflinger, a strong, sturdy pony, has a gold coat and a pale mane and tail.

PALOMINO horses, although a colour type and not a breed of pony, must conform to certain standards, and so deserve special mention. In the United States the Palomino varies from 14·2 to 15·3 hands, while in Britain there are show classes for Palomino stock of all heights. This glorious colouring is said to have originated in Spain, where such an animal was known as 'Ysabella' or 'Isabella' after the queen who favoured them. It is possible too that the chariot horses of the ancient Greeks, described by them as *xanthos* ('shining like the sun'), were also of this elusive shade. The body colour of the Palomino is like a bright gold coin, gleaming and metallic, and the mane and tail are of pure white hair. At birth, however, the foals are very pale cream, and the adults revert to this juvenile colouring during the winter, only regaining their golden glory as the summer coat comes through.

There are Palomino Welsh, Palomino Shetlands, Palomino part-bred Arabians and so on, and the conformation for each must comply with that breed's standard. Because the colour usually deepens with age, there are two registers for British Palominos, one for animals up to six years of age, and a permanent one for those six years and over. To gain acceptance, the Palominos are inspected by officials, and must achieve certain standards before registration is granted.

Finally we look at a golden chestnut pony with a light mane and tail. This is the HAFLINGER, a strong mountain breed originally bred for pack purposes in the South Tyrol. Although it is a strong and sturdy pony, it does show the influence of Arabian bloodlines, and is often described as being 'a prince in front and a peasant behind'. About 14 hands high, the overall appearance of the Haflinger is one of strength and safety, and in the regions of its birth it has been used for years to move loads of hay and timber in summer, and to haul sleighs during the heavy snows of winter. Its generous temperament and sure-footed stride has made it popular for trekking, and it has been exported to many countries of the world as an ideal ride-and-drive utility pony. Its thick winter coat enables it to live out even in the most inclement weather, and it is a hardworking, economical pony that is gaining in popularity.

Caring for Your Pony

When you have acquired your pony, you will either keep it in a field at all times, when it is said to be 'at grass', or you may prefer to keep it stabled, housed in a comfortable loose box and regularly exercised. Some ponies do best when kept outside in the summer and inside during the winter months. Ponies at grass need different care to those which are stabled, as well as different foodstuffs.

For a pony at grass it is essential to have sufficient grazing, and these areas must be adequately fenced. Wooden post-and-rail fencing is by far the best for containing ponies, but it is expensive to erect and maintain in good condition. A wooden fence has specially treated posts sunk into the ground; then the rails are either slotted or nailed into place. The best fences have three rows of rails, and are regularly treated with preservative. As a cheaper alternative to post-and-rails, it is possible to use three tautly stretched strands of tough wire in conjunction with wooden posts set in the ground at intervals of 12 feet (3.5 m). Some ponies are very destructive to fencing, stretching over the top strand of wire to get at the grass on the other side, and it may be necessary to use barbed wire for the top strand to prevent this. If such wire is used it must be expertly stretched and properly fixed as serious accidents can occur when it becomes loose and sags. Many fields are already enclosed with old hedges, and these provide a good weather break for the pony. Before putting the animal into such a field however, it is essential to test every bit of the hedge for thin or weak areas which may need reinforcing with posts and wire. All reinforcements to fencing should be nailed from inside so that the pony, pushing against the top rail or wire, puts the strain against the posts and not on the nails alone.

Ponies at grass need lots of lush grazing in well-fenced, sheltered fields.

Right: Foals in particular need safe fencing, and for small pony breeds wire mesh can be added to prevent accidents.

Above: Barbed wire makes a totally unsuitable and potentially dangerous barrier for any pony.

Far right: A proper gate is essential and may be of the traditional wooden variety, like this one, or of tubular metal.

The gate is just as important as the fencing and the best type is a special field gate of timber or metal, not less than 4 feet (1·2 m) in width and opening in towards the field. The latch must be pony-proof, and this and the gate's hinges must be kept well oiled at all times. It is important to be able to open the gate easily with one hand so that you do not have any trouble taking your pony in and out of the field. If the field is some way from your home, it is advisable to secure the gate with a length of chain and a self-locking padlock. If a combination lock is used, you do not have to worry about losing the key; you just need to choose an easily remembered combination code. Gateways quickly become churned up to form a sea of mud during very wet weather, especially if the soil is a heavy clay. It is very wise to pre-empt this situation by arranging, well before winter sets in, for about 1 foot (0·3 m) of earth to be dug out and replaced by tamped-down hardcore, chalk, gravel or coarse ash.

The grass in your field should be lush and green, without too much clover. You must check it carefully for poisonous plants and other hazards such as old tin cans, broken glass and wire. One pony needs 2·5 acres (1 hectare) of grazing and this area is more easily managed if it is divided into two sections which may be alternately grazed. If necessary, you may use electric fencing for this division, but it must be properly erected and maintained. Grass grows from the middle of spring until early autumn, and reaches its maximum food value during the midsummer months. It is best to use the most sheltered section of your field for the winter months, saving the other plot for early spring. The winter plot takes at least eight weeks to recover and begin growing its spring crop, but it is helped if it can be rolled and harrowed by tractor.

During a very wet winter the pony may have churned up the ground, leaving deep impressions of its hooves. This is known as *poaching* the ground and, if the damage is severe, it is worth sowing some grass seed and a little fertilizer when the harrowing is done. The pony must not be allowed on the land during such treatment. To keep limited grazing in good condition, you should take the trouble to collect the pony's droppings at regular intervals, adding them to your manure heap. At the same time, a lookout can be kept for an invasion of toxic plants, and areas of coarse grass can be cut down to allow more tender succulent shoots to develop.

Right: A pony must have sufficient water, and if there is no piped supply, it must be carried and poured into a suitable drinking receptacle.

These tough pony foals will winter out, protected from north winds by a sheltering wall.

One of the most important things to establish in your pony's paddock is an adequate water supply. If there is no system of piped water, it is a good idea to have a channel dug to carry a reinforced hosepipe from the nearest tap, underground, to the field. Unless buried, it will freeze in winter, just at the most trying time for carrying heavy buckets of water. Always disconnect the hose after filling the pony's water tank, and never leave the end of the hose in the tank as it may act as a siphon and drain the water back out again. The best type of drinking tank is of galvanized metal or industrial-weight plastic – much better than buckets which do not hold enough water and are easily knocked over by the pony. It must not be too tall or your pony will not be able to drink comfortably, and if it is too large you will have problems in trying to tip the water out before giving the tank its regular cleaning. The tank should be scrubbed out at least once every three months, using clean water and a stiff brush to remove all the algae. Stubborn marks can be lifted with a weak solution of household bleach in cold water. Never site the tank under a tree where falling leaves or the droppings of roosting birds may pollute the water.

If your pony is to winter out in its field, you may feel happier if it has a shelter. High hedges protect ponies from fierce winds and driving rain, and fields in exposed conditions may have windbreaks at strategic points, made from sheep hurdles set at angles and reinforced with straw bales. Such shelters must be carefully built for strength and the straw bales must be protected from the weather by polythene and by wire fencing from the attentions of the pony which may try to pull fodder from the bales. A proper wooden field shelter, carefully sited to be cosy and draught-free, can be built on a tamped chalk or concrete base. The floor should extend well beyond the entrance to prevent the building being filled with mud in wet weather, and should gently slope away to provide adequate drainage. It is a good idea to fix brackets on the open side of the shelter to take two long poles which may act as a temporary gate whenever it is necessary to confine the pony to the shelter. However, you must never tie up your pony or confine it in a three-sided building for any length of time because it may get chilled. The animal should be free to use the shelter as and when it wishes to find protection from cold and damp. A well-fed pony which has been allowed to grow a natural winter coat will never suffer unduly from cold conditions if it can exercise freely, but a pony which becomes saturated with rain and is then subjected to long periods of cold may suffer a chill.

The shelter should be kept fresh and clean, with the droppings being picked up regularly. Hay should be fed in a tidy rack and clean buckets for hard feed and water should be placed in wall holders. There should be a mineral lick, also in a wall holder, and, in summer, an impregnated fly-killing strip may be hung from the ceiling.

In winter, a pony with a full natural coat should be only lightly groomed, otherwise the grease in its coat, designed to keep in warmth, will be removed. For light hacking, the mane and tail are brushed well and attention is paid to

Hardy breeds grow extra long manes and thick double coats to keep them protected from the worst of winter weather.

Thin-coated ponies can be fitted with special New Zealand-style rugs to protect them during their exercise periods in the paddock.

the feet and heels, cleaning off mud, checking the shoes, drying the legs well around the fetlocks and pasterns and oiling the hooves. Any dried mud should be removed, and careful attention paid to any areas of the head and body where the tack is fitted. After gentle riding, the pony must be returned to the field only after it has completely cooled down, and it will probably go immediately to the muddiest patch to roll.

If the pony that lives out is required to undertake any strenuous work, such as hunting, during the winter months, it may be trace-clipped which helps to prevent undue sweating during exercise. The hair is clipped away from the underside of the neck, the belly, between the forelegs and the girth area, using special clippers which need expert handling. A pony clipped in this way needs the added protection of a New Zealand rug and, before this is fitted, the unclipped areas of its coat must be thoroughly cleaned and groomed. A New Zealand rug is made of tough canvas or nylon material, wind and water-proofed, lined with wool or quilted fabric for warmth and has special straps which prevent the rug from slipping or coming off even if the pony rolls vigor-ously. It is vital that this type of rug fits really well so that there is no chance of the pony getting caught up by any of the tough straps.

The rug must be taken off every day and the lining brushed, and the pony is generally groomed before the rug is replaced. A New Zealand rug is not suit-able for use in the stable as its waterproof qualities make it act rather like a sweat suit, not allowing perspiration to escape. For this reason also, the rug must never be put on a hot or sweating pony.

Even if you are not riding the pony in winter, it is important to feed it twice a day and to check that the water has not iced over. Hay should be fed in the rack or, if you have no shelter, in a hay net tied to a convenient branch or post. If you are riding, extra food, perhaps in the form of special cubes, should also be given, the quantity being determined by the amount of work being done. Cubes should never be fed on the ground as they are comparatively ex-pensive and the pony will waste them. A hot bran mash is appreciated by most ponies after a hard day's work, and a little freshly boiled and cooled lin-seed jelly may be added occasionally for periods of two or three weeks to im-prove the animal's condition.

In summer, it may be necessary to restrict the pony's grazing if the grass is thick and lush. The best way to do this is to keep it in the field shelter, or stable, during the day, turning it out again to graze through the night. This prevents overweight, and the possibility of laminitis (see chapter *An A–Z of Pony Health*), and also keeps it free from biting flies and other annoying insects. Even though there is plenty of nourishing food for your pony, you should still visit the field at least twice every day to check that all is well, and that there is adequate water. When flies are particularly bad, special repellent creams may be applied to the pony's skin and a fringed browband can be attached to its headcollar. Two ponies living together may be seen standing head to tail in summer, each brushing flies from the other's face with its swishing tail.

The pony's summer coat is generally fine and close-lying and therefore quite easy to groom. If you take part in gymkhanas or other competitions, you should get your pony as fit as possible by gradually increasing the riding sessions and giving supplementary food in the form of cubes at least an hour before riding. Groom the animal carefully before and after riding to help tone up the muscles, as well as improving its appearance.

If your pony is difficult to catch, it should wear a well-fitting headcollar all the time it is turned out in the field. This may be of leather or woven nylon and must have good quality buckles. A badly fitted headcollar can be danger-ous as the pony can get it caught on the fence or gate or, worse still, might inadvertently put its foot through the straps while grazing or scratching. Ponies that are very naughty about being caught can have a short length of rope tied to the headcollar which gives you something to grab when you eventually get the animal cornered. Ponies must be encouraged to come when called, and the best way to achieve this is to feed the pony only when it responds by advancing towards you. You should make a point of catching the pony at all sorts of irregular times, even if it is just to walk it a few steps on the leading rope, giving a reward and then releasing it again. Ponies which dis-like being caught are generally those who relate it with having to work hard, and so it is up to you to re-educate the animal with patience and kindness.

Below: Hay should never be fed on the ground as much of it will be wasted.

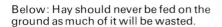

Left: Most ponies roll in wet mud which dries on their coats, acting as a protective covering.

To catch your pony, go into the field and call it by name. If it refuses to come, try kneeling on the ground. Do not go walking straight up to the pony, but go forward a few steps, then let the pony take a few steps towards you. Eventually you will be in a position to clip the leading rope onto the rear link of the headcollar and lead the pony forward. Always walk alongside your pony, holding the rope with your right hand a few inches below the animal's chin, with the end of the rope in your other hand for extra safety. When going through a gate or doorway, pass through ahead of your pony, otherwise you could get squeezed up against the doorjamb or gatepost and be hurt. To turn the pony out into the field, first make sure that it is cool and not sweating up. Go into the field and turn the pony's head towards you, carefully close the gate, then release the rope before giving a cube or carrot as a reward. Never encourage the pony to gallop off for this might result in your getting accidentally kicked.

Winter or summer, the pony must have its feet cared for. The foot is made up of layers of insensitive, constantly growing horn, and within this tough outer box-like structure are the soft *laminae* which surround the bones of the foot. If you lift up a pony's hoof and look underneath it, the visible part is the horny sole which covers an inner sensitive sole. The large wedge-shaped structure extending in from the heel is called the *frog*, and this should touch the ground, acting as an anti-slip aid and a shock absorber. The hardness of hooves varies considerably in ponies, some needing very regular shoeing to prevent damage to their rather soft or brittle feet, while others, notably those from Caspian stock, may never need iron shoes. Shod or not, the feet still require the regular attention of the blacksmith or farrier, as feet allowed to grow over-long develop splits and cracks in the horn and may give rise to long periods of lameness and distress.

The grass-fed pony has a short fine coat in summer, and is quite easy to groom, ready for gymkhana and show events.

Right: A well-fitted head-collar may be left on your pony to make it easier to catch.

A rope is clipped on in order to lead the pony out of the field.

A pony out at grass should have its feet inspected before being ridden out and any mud or stones must be removed with a special hoof pick. The outside of the hoof should be brushed clean and the heels checked for any sign of cracking or sponginess. Either of these conditions should be treated by cleaning and drying the heels, then applying a suitable veterinary ointment. An unpleasant smell emanating from the bottom of the foot usually indicates a condition known as *thrush* which should receive professional treatment.

The farrier, or blacksmith, is one of your pony's best and most needed friends, for care of the feet is all important and must never be neglected. Your local farrier may have his forge near enough to your home for you to take the pony along for attention about every two months. If not, you must arrange for the smith to visit you on a regular basis and it is often necessary to book up well in advance. It is better to arrange for the farrier to visit a whole group of ponies gathered together at one venue for a joint 'shoeing day'. This is more convenient for the blacksmith and may work out to be a little cheaper per pony.

41

There are two methods of shoeing a pony. The traditional method is *hot shoeing* in which the farrier makes an individual shoe for each of the pony's feet, heating each one in his forge fire and hammering it on an anvil until it is exactly right. In *cold shoeing*, ready-made sets of shoes are used and the farrier chooses those which best fit the pony's feet. It is obvious that hot shoeing is the best method, but it is not always easy to find a farrier that will do it.

The first thing the farrier does when shoeing a pony is to cut away the *clenches* (bend-over nails) which hold on the shoe; then he levers off the old shoe with large pincers. The sole and frog are cleaned out and the foot is re-shaped by paring away any overgrowth of horn. Neglected feet have very long and jagged parts removed with a special horn cutter, then a rasp is employed to level the bottom of the foot. In hot shoeing, once the shoe has been fashioned to fit the hoof and is complete with clip and nail holes, it is heated in the fire once more. When applied to the bottom of the hoof, it sears the horn and makes it easy to see whether or not it is a perfect fit. If not, further adjustments are made, but if it does fit, the hot shoe is then plunged into cold water to cool and temper it.

Special nails are used to fix the shoes to the pony's feet and these must be placed with extreme care so that they only penetrate the insensitive parts of the hoof walls. The protruding ends of the nails are twisted off, then the tips are rasped down and hammered flat to form the clenches. Finally the farrier taps the shoe lightly all round and rasps the join between the shoe and the hoof to finish off.

The stabled pony needs a roomy loose box in which to live which must be of sound construction, well ventilated and with a wide, two-sectioned, outward opening door. The door itself should be hung on well-oiled hinges and be fitted with proper bolts, designed to prevent clever ponies from letting themselves out when the mood takes them. Most loose boxes are made of timber, while others may be constructed of bricks or blocks, and all should have impervious floors of brick or concrete that will drain well. Any windows must be covered by bars or mesh to protect them from being broken by the pony, and should allow some ventilation either with louvres or with a top-opening pane.

The loose box should have a few essential fittings on the wall. A special ring fitted at the pony's chest-level is useful for tying it up while the box is being mucked out, and another, this time at eye-level, can be used during grooming

The blacksmith tries a shoe for size.

Left: The pony kept in, or stabled, must have sufficient exercise and plenty to think about so that it does not become bored.

The hinges and bolts of the loosebox door must be kept well-oiled and in good condition.

for *short-racking* the pony. This merely means tying the rope from the head-collar closely to the ring to prevent the animal moving about unduly. This ring may also be used for tying up a haynet if required, or hay may be fed in a special metal rack fitted to the wall. Such a rack must be raised to about the level of the pony's head; if it is higher, hay seeds or dust may get into the pony's eyes, and if it is too low, the hay will be lifted out and strewn all over the box, wasting much of it. You should never feed hay on the floor of the box as this will be scattered about and trodden on and then the pony will reject it as food. If there is no manger, metal holders fitted at chest-level containing buckets for food and water again help to prevent wastage of hard feed. The buckets should be kept clean, so it is wise to invest in a spare set.

Wheat straw makes the finest bedding for your pony, but it is possible to use other straw, wood shavings, peat or even shredded paper. If you use oat straw, you may find that your pony eats it. Soiled straw from the box can be made into a manure heap and, when rotted down, has value as fertilizer, but soiled wood shavings or paper are worthless. To bed down your pony, take the baled straw into the box and cut the cord which binds it, rolling this up for disposal later. Never leave this string in the box as it may prove dangerous to your pony. The very compressed straw must be shaken out with a fork to separate all the pieces and must then be spread in a thick layer all over the floor of the loose box. The bed needs to be deep and comfortable, a little higher around the walls of the box for warmth and for protection against possible injury as the pony gets up and down. If shavings or paper are used, you must take care to ensure that they come from reliable sources, are clean and uncontaminated by rat droppings. Such material must be spread as a very deep bed to prevent bare areas resulting from the pony's movements around the box. When peat is used, a thick layer is put in the box at the beginning; wet areas are removed each day and fresh peat added; then the whole box is cleared out completely at the end of the winter. Only boxes with perfect

Hay should be fed from a rack, or a net at the level of the pony's head.

drainage should be used for this method of deep litter bedding, otherwise they soon smell strongly of ammonia and may become unhealthy and therefore unusable.

Mucking out the stable must be a daily routine, unless the deep litter system is used, and you will need a sturdy wheelbarrow, a shovel, a stable fork, a stiff broom and a sheet made of plastic, canvas or hessian. A wicker or plastic basket is also useful. First thing each morning you may either remove the pony from the loose box or short-rack it to eat a small feed of hay while the clean straw is separated from the droppings. The stable fork is used for this job, the clean straw being heaped around the sides of the box while the droppings and wet, soiled bedding are placed in the barrow. When the centre of the box is clear, the broom is used to brush up the soiled particles remaining, and these are also shovelled into the barrow. The remaining straw can be left to dry out around the sides of the box and the bare central area allowed to air during the morning. The pony may be untied unless it is to be exercised, and the barrow is wheeled to the manure heap to be emptied.

At midday the bedding is spread over the floor once more as some ponies like to lie down to rest in the early afternoon. A little fresh straw is added to replace that which was soiled, and care should be taken to see that all the straws are well tossed and lie in different directions as this makes the springiest and most comfortable bed. Loose straw should always be carried in the plastic, canvas or hessian sheet to prevent odd bits scattering around outside and looking untidy. Any loose straw or debris outside the box should be regularly swept up and added to the manure heap. In the evening, the basket or *skep* is taken into the box to collect the afternoon's droppings, and these too are disposed of on the manure heap.

The manure heap is made by marking out a convenient square or rectangle in a spare, well-drained corner of your grounds. It should be somewhere easily reached with the wheelbarrow whatever the weather, for a laden barrow is too heavy to push through mud during the winter months. Start by laying the soiled straw and droppings around the perimeter of your heap, then fill in the centre. Wearing rubber boots, walk on the surface of the heap each day to compress the material, and when the heap becomes too high to reach easily, start making a new one. After nine months, the matured heap is ready for use as an excellent garden fertilizer, and two-year-old manure heaps reach the consistency of fine peat and may be forked or spread on pasture to enrich the soil.

At Pony Club camp, ponies soon make themselves 'at home' in temporary accommodation.

Correct feeding is very important for the stabled pony, and the amount of each feed depends greatly on the animal's size and how much energy is expended during the work it is required to carry out each day. Advice on feeding is beyond the scope of this book, but the following hints may be of help. It may be most convenient for you to feed specially formulated cubes, rather than mixing your own feeds of various cereals, to supplement the hay ration. Hay is nutritious and provides the bulk of the pony's food. It is made by farmers during the summer months by cutting and drying grass at its peak growing time when it contains the maximum amount of vitamins and minerals, and the cheapest way to obtain your hay is to buy it 'off the field'. By doing this you will have seen the growing crop and will know that it does not contain any unwanted weeds or poisonous plants such as ragwort, and you will also be able to keep a check on the haymaking, seeing that it is turned and dried well before baling, and that there have been no heavy rains since cutting which may cause the final product to grow mildew in the bales. Remember to keep hay for at least six months before feeding it to your pony. When you approach the farmer, you may ask for the hay to be delivered from the field to your storage area, or you may save even more money by arranging collection with your own transport. Buying stored hay in small quantities is much more expensive.

A stabled pony must be thoroughly groomed each day, ensuring cleanliness and promoting good health and condition. A special grooming kit is important and consists of a hoof pick, a stiff dandy brush, a finer body brush, a curry comb of metal or rubber, a mane comb, two different coloured sponges, a shaped water brush, a stable rubber, some hoof oil and a brush, and a plastic holder, basket or bucket in which to carry the kit. First, collect your kit and a bucket of water. Catch up and tie up the pony, either in the box to its

This pony has been expertly groomed and gleams with good health as he is led from his loosebox.

45

high ring, or outside if it is a warm sunny day. Picking up each foot in turn, ·use the hoof pick to clean from the heel towards the toe and down the wedges of the frog. Take care to avoid pricking the frog, and test the shoe to check that it is not loose and that the clenches are still flat against the wall of the hoof. If your pony is quiet, place the skep you have for mucking out under each foot as you clean it out, thus preventing the debris from falling on the floor or the box. Next use the dandy brush and, starting at the head, work all over the near side of the pony, removing any flecks of dirt, dust and loose hairs. This brush is very harsh and must be used gently in the direction of the coat. Work down the neck, shoulder and foreleg, then down the nearside of the sides and flanks, over the hips and down the hindleg, then pass round to the other side. Push the mane over and out of the way while you brush down the neck then continue down that side of the body and legs. Next use the body brush and go all over the pony again. This brush reaches right through the hairs, cleaning the coat as well as stimulating circulation in the skin. Use it with a firm, smooth stroke and, after four or five such movements, clean the brush with the curry comb held in the other hand and tap the curry comb smartly against the inside of the skep to dislodge the dirt.

After strenuous exercise, mud and sweat may be cleaned off the pony by sponging or a gentle hosing if the weather is fine.

Left: Make sure your sponge is spotlessly clean before you use it to wipe your pony's eyes.

The mane and tail should be brushed through with the body brush only, as the dandy brush may break the hairs, and then the mane thoroughly combed with the mane comb. Moisten a sponge and use it to wipe the eyes; then rinse it and use it to wipe out the nostrils. Finally rinse thoroughly once more and use to clean the lips if necessary. A sponge of a different colour (for identification) should be moistened and used to clean out the dock area. The water brush, lightly moistened, is used to lay the hairs of the mane and the root of the tail into place, then a tail bandage may be applied if desired. The same brush is used to wash the feet unless the weather is very cold. While the feet are drying, a folded stable rubber, which is a rectangular linen cloth, may be used to bang and stroke the pony's coat, raising a glossy sheen and removing any last vestiges of dust. When dry, the hooves may be painted with a thin coat of oil.

Clipped ponies are fitted with specially shaped rugs. During the night, a robust rug made of jute or hemp is ideal, kept in place with a padded roller which fits around the girth, and for extra warmth, thick woollen blankets may be put on underneath the night rug. During the day, smarter rugs are more usual, made of lightweight wool or quilted nylon. These rugs may have your initials appliquéd in the corners, and you can obtain matching leg bandages for your pony. The rugs must always be put on carefully to avoid any creases, and the straps must be buckled up firmly but not tight enough to cut off the circulation. The undersides of the rugs must be aired daily and brushed free from dust and hair. A well-cared-for pony is a credit to its owner and repays all the work and good feeding by looking well and working happily.

Above: Apply a thin coat of oil with a brush to keep your pony's hooves in good condition.

An A~Z of Pony Health

Ponies are rarely ill, but you must remember that it is very important to call the veterinary surgeon for help, advice and treatment whenever you suspect a severe injury or the onset of disease. A healthy pony has clear bright eyes and pricked ears, its coat is glossy and lies smooth and flat. The skin is supple, the appetite is normal and the pony takes an interest in its surroundings. On the other hand a sick pony stands with lowered head and looks dejected; its eyes are dull and its ears are drooping or held back. Its coat is dull and staring and the skin is tight and hard. The animal may breathe irregularly and refuse its food.

The temperature of a pony at rest should be from 99°F to 101°F (37.2°C to 38.3°C) but may vary according to age, type and food of the animal. Its pulse rate is 40 to 45 beats per minute, and the younger the animal the quicker the rate.

ABSCESSES are localized collections of pus, often the results of bruising or a fall. Acute abscesses, if left alone, eventually break and discharge themselves. Such an abscess forms a 'point' before bursting and this process may be hastened by the applications of hot fomentations. In the case of a chronic abscess, the veterinary surgeon should be consulted for it will need opening and draining to allow slow healing from within. Antibiotic treatment generally speeds the healing process.

BLEEDING often looks more alarming than it is. If from a vein it is known as venous bleeding and may be stopped by applying the ball of the thumb to the wound and pressing hard for a few minutes until the flow stops and the blood has clotted. If from an artery, it is known as arterial bleeding and is serious. If the artery is severed, try to draw the edges of the wound together and bandage tightly until the veterinary surgeon arrives. Prevent the pony from moving. Venous blood is dark in colour and flows rather slowly, but continuously and congeals quite quickly. Arterial blood is very bright and flows in spurts, being pumped by the heart.

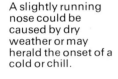

A slightly running nose could be caused by dry weather or may herald the onset of a cold or chill.

A pony in good health has bright eyes and a smooth, glossy coat.

BOTS are the larvae of the gadfly which lays its eggs on the skin of the pony, generally on the legs, shoulders and flanks. The pony licks the eggs and the larvae penetrate the mucous membranes of the gums, lips and tongue. They undergo periods of moulting, and then move to the animal's stomach where they remain for about nine months. A pony heavily infested with bots quickly loses condition, has a staring coat (that is, when all the hairs are standing away from the skin) and may have a staggering gait. It may be either con-stipated or have diarrhoea and may be very restless, stamping its feet and kicking at its belly. It is possible to prevent infestation by bots by keeping the pony in during the active periods of the gadfly, and by meticulously grooming away any eggs seen attached to the animal's skin. Some preparations for worming a pony also contain ingredients which will destroy and disperse any larvae in the body.

BRAN MASH is given to sick ponies. It is made by filling a bucket two-thirds full with broad bran; then pour a little boiling water onto this and stir with a wooden spoon until the bran is wetted evenly through. Cover the bucket with a clean teatowel and leave it until cool to feed to the pony. Making a perfect bran mash takes lots of practice for it is impossible to say exactly how much water one should add. When properly made the mash should be sweet and crumble-dry, neither stiff and sticky nor wet and gruel-like. It is ready to feed when you are able to put your bare hand right into the mash without being burned. For a treat, or to encourage a sick pony to eat, add a little brown sugar, treacle or molasses to the mash, or perhaps a few oats or some shredded apple or carrot.

BROKEN KNEES are caused when a pony falls heavily on a hard road. The con-dition may range from a mere scraping off of the hair without badly breaking the skin, to very deep wounds. In the former case, the knees must be gently bathed with mild antiseptic in warm water, and this must be done daily until the wounds heal, when the hair will begin to grow back over the abraded areas. With deep or extensive cuts veterinary treatment is essential and an anti-tetanus injection may also be necessary. Permanent hairless scars may result from such accidents, so great care should always be taken when riding along roads or on other hard surfaces.

COLIC is a severe tummy-ache caused in the pony by a variety of things such as unsuitable food or a chill. In a mild case the pony seems very unhappy and looks round at its flanks, often kicking up at its belly with a hindleg. In an acute case the pony will throw itself down and may become violently agi-tated, kicking and sweating. The veterinary surgeon should be called without delay in all cases of colic and he will administer a soothing injection. While waiting for his arrival you should walk the pony around and keep it as calm as possible. Try to prevent it from throwing itself down but, if it does go down, do not allow it to roll violently as there is a risk of it twisting a gut. You may administer colic mixture, from your first aid kit, as a drench (*see below*).

COUGHS can be very serious, and the first thing to do when your pony develops one is to stop riding immediately, for riding a pony with a bad cough can cause broken wind. Ponies which live out seem to throw off coughs more quickly than those which are stabled. Various types of liquid cough cures are prescribed which are mixed with the pony's favourite food.

A pony may lick eggs of the gadfly from its legs and flanks during the summer months.

A pony that stands for long periods in muddy conditions could develop cracked heels.

Right: This mare and foal are in a field that has been invaded by ragwort, a highly toxic plant.

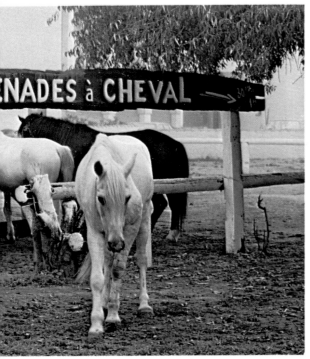

This Camargue Pony has injured itself badly and is very lame.

CRACKED HEELS are sore areas on the heels and at the back of the pastern. Sometimes the sores spread to the coronet and the pony may go very lame. The condition is often caused by the pony standing for long periods in wet and muddy conditions. Preventive measures include leaving the heels untrimmed in wet, cold weather, and treatment consists of daily cleansing of the affected areas before applying a soothing antiseptic ointment.

DRENCHING is the giving of liquid medicines to the pony by means of a special drenching bottle. It is important to be shown the correct way to administer a drench so that you are in no danger of choking the pony.

FIRST AID KITS should contain a pair of blunt-nosed scissors, several bandages of various widths, several rolls of cotton wool, packets of lint or sterile dressing, a bottle of colic mixture from the veterinary surgeon, saline solution in a spray bottle, a puffer pack of antibiotic powder, Epsom salts, glycerine, antiseptic ointments and kaolin paste. The kit should be kept clean and readily to hand, stored perhaps in a small cupboard or a large box or tin with a well-fitting lid. Everyone in the family should know where to find the kit, and when any of the contents are used they should be replaced without delay.

GIRTH GALLS are caused by an ill-fitting or dirty girth and are more likely to occur when a pony is in a soft, unfit condition. When a pony is started into work after being turned out, at first it is better to use a well-adjusted nylon girth to prevent rubbing. If a gall does develop it should be cleaned and treated with an antiseptic ointment containing cortisone and the pony must not be ridden again until it has completely healed. It is possible to toughen up intact skin in the girth area by rubbing with surgical or methylated spirit, and ponies in soft condition may have their girths padded with a soft material, or encased in rubber tubing.

LAMENESS in the pony may be due to any one of many causes and the first thing to do is to determine which leg is affected. This is generally done by trotting out the pony in hand. Having found the affected leg it must be examined carefully to find any area of pain, heat or swelling. As most cases of lameness occur in the foot, this is checked first and compared with the foot of the opposite leg. Lameness may be caused by a stone wedged between the shoe and the frog, a pricked sole or several other reasons. If you cannot see the problem then you must seek professional advice. There are various treatments for lameness; a poultice may be required, or you may have to run cool water through a hosepipe down the affected limb (*see* TUBBING).

LAMINITIS is fever of the feet and is excruciatingly painful for a pony. It develops most readily in small ponies that very rapidly put on weight when allowed too much lush early grass. A pony with laminitis stands on its heels with the hind feet well under the body to take its weight. The animal is in obvious pain and very reluctant to move. Send for the veterinary surgeon for emergency treatment, get the farrier to remove the shoes, and restrict the pony's food. Standing the pony in cold water or hosepiping the legs and feet may help to reduce the pain a little. Old ponies must have their grazing restricted in the spring and early summer if they are not being worked. Remember that a pony that has once had laminitis is very prone to getting it again.

OVER-REACH INJURIES occur when the pony's hind toe strikes the back of a foreleg with a downward, slicing action, causing an unpleasant wound. It happens most often in jumping and out hunting as the animal tires or is pulled up suddenly and unexpectedly. The injured leg should be carefully bathed and cleaned before applying antibiotic powder from a puffer pack. A thick cotton wool pad may be applied, held in place by a light bandage. Change the dressing frequently and rest the pony until the wound had completely healed.

POISONOUS PLANTS abound in the countryside and some may be fatal if eaten by the pony. Perhaps the most common is the RAGWORT, easily overlooked before it reaches its flowering stage. Luckily, few ponies will eat it as a growing plant, and when the bright yellow daisy-like flowers open it is easily identified, pulled out and burned. This plant is most toxic to the horse family after it has withered and dried out, so it is important to ensure that it does not get into the pony's hay. DEADLY NIGHTSHADE twines innocently in the hedgerows, and tall stately spears of the COMMON FOXGLOVE abound in shady corners. Both are highly toxic, and so are RHODODENRON, PRIVET and IVY. Perhaps most dangerous of all is the YEW, which ponies seem to find attractive and which may prove fatal, even if eaten in quite small amounts. Other dangerous plants are GREEN BRACKEN, BOX, LABURNUM, LUPIN and LAUREL, all of which are at their most hazardous as they start to wilt and dry out. Many people feed garden trimmings to ponies, thinking to supplement their grazing, and such well-meaning actions can cost ponies' lives as the clippings ferment in the animals' stomachs causing severe colic and probably death. As prevention is better than cure, the pony's paddock should be searched regularly for poisonous plants, and all neighbouring gardeners should be visited in a friendly way and told that the pony must not be fed clippings or trimmings of any description. If poisoning is suspected at any time, the veterinary surgeon must be called without delay for emergency treatment of the pony.

This foal is having a good scratch, and should be inspected to make sure that he is not harbouring any parasites, or has any form of skin disease.

It is particularly important to keep ponies parasite-free when they are handled and petted by small children.

53

POULTICING consists of making a hot poultice usually of kaolin paste, heated by standing the opened tin in almost boiling water for some time. The hot paste is spread with a knife onto a piece of lint of suitable size to cover the affected area. The temperature is tested by applying the lint to the back of your wrist: it should feel very hot but must not burn. Apply to the area and hold in place with a heat-retaining bandage. Change the poultice regularly, repeating the treatment until the wound is clean or the swelling has subsided.

PUSTULAR DERMATITIS is a skin condition generally found in the region where the saddle and girth fit the pony. It is an infectious disease and may be spread by the use of infected grooming equipment and saddlery, or in stable dust. It is first noticed as small round areas of bare skin, and is treated with specially prescribed veterinary ointment until the lesions disappear. Care must be taken to contain the disease and all equipment must be kept as clean as possible, the infected pony having only his own brushes used for grooming his coat.

RINGWORM is a fungus infection and highly contagious, first noticed when circles of bare skin appear. When the disease is confirmed the pony must be isolated and the affected areas treated with a special fungicidal lotion. All rugs, saddlery and grooming equipment must be cleaned, disinfected and treated with a fungicide, too, until all signs of the disease have disappeared. Great care must be taken in washing the hands carefully after treating the pony, and all the pony's bedding should be burned rather than being put on the manure heap in the usual way.

SWEET ITCH is an unpleasant skin condition caused by the allergic reaction of a pony to small biting insects such as midges, to some pollens or, in some cases, to sunlight. Midges are active from one hour before sunset until one hour after, so if your pony is prone to this complaint it is advisable to bring it into the stable during that period every day. The stable should be treated with fly spray and the pony may be rubbed with a repellent. If the pony is not helped in this way, it will rub the itching areas of its body until they are raw, and must have a veterinary ointment regularly applied to soothe and heal the affected regions.

TETANUS is prevented in the pony by the administration of a yearly injection. Tetanus germs abound in the soil and may gain access to the pony's body through any cut or graze; the awful disease develops after about ten days and is often fatal. If your pony has not been vaccinated and suffers a cut or injury, a special serum may be given for its protection, but it is much better to have the annual precautionary dose of Tetanus Toxoid. People who work with animals might also consider having themselves vaccinated against the disease and should discuss a vaccination programme with their doctors.

TUBBING is a method of easing swelling or pain in the pony's feet or lower legs and is an alternative to hosepiping. It consists of putting, in a tall bucket, an antiseptic solution in water of the desired temperature, and placing the pony's affected foot in this to soak. The temperature of the solution may be regulated by adding hot or cold water as desired.

WARBLES are recognizable as lumps showing clearly under the pony's skin, indicating the presence of a large maggot which is the larva of the warble fly. While it is growing, the maggot must not be disturbed, but eventually it will make a small hole in the skin and climb through to the outside world. If the maggot is killed under the skin, a permanent, thickened lump may form which may be unsightly and, if in the saddle region, uncomfortable for the pony. Warbles are often found in the saddle region, and the pony must not be ridden until each lump is seen to have an exit hole. These are then treated with antibiotic powder to prevent any infection entering the small wounds.

WORMS are a constant problem with ponies which reinfect themselves with larvae during normal grazing. While a normal healthy pony can carry a small worm burden, if it gets sick or has too many of the parasites, its health will quickly deteriorate and it will soon look very ill indeed. A pony with a

Ponies at grass during summer are prone to attack by the warble fly.

heavy worm load looks rather thin and has a dull, staring coat. The pony may be host to several different varieties of worms and the best way to overcome the problem is to collect a small fresh sample of its dung, pop it into a clean plastic bag or small glass jar and take it to your veterinary surgeon for examination. The microscope allows identification of the worms present and the correct dose of an effective vermifuge will be prescribed, the dose possibly consisting of a measured quantity of powder. Withhold your pony's feed until you know that it is really hungry, then add the powder to a small amount of its favourite meal, such as oats or bran. A spoonful of brown sugar sprinkled on top should also make the meal quite irresistible. Once a worming routine has been established, it is a good policy to continue to give correct doses of the medicine at regular intervals throughout the year. If the pony is very difficult to dose and refuses to take the powders in its food, ask your veterinary surgeon for a more palatable treatment, or one given in semi-liquid form by means of a long plastic syringe.

Below: Regular worming treatment is essential for all ponies, and must be done under veterinary supervision.

Right: Prevention is better than cure, and this is especially true in pony care. These superb polo ponies are heavily bandaged to protect their limbs against knocks and strains.

56

Enjoying Your Pony

When learning to ride it is important that you receive expert tuition, for bad habits are easily formed and may prove difficult to break. There are many excellent RIDING SCHOOLS, some of which may even allow you to take lessons mounted on your own pony if it is considered suitable for the job. Even riders of long standing may benefit from occasional courses of riding lessons to correct little faults and improve technique, and to include, perhaps, advanced riding such as dressage or eventing. Riding establishments also help you to learn how to school and produce your pony for showing, jumping or gymkhanas and will help to prepare you and your pony for a day's hunting.

RIDING AND PONY CLUBS also exist and provide opportunities for riders and their horses or ponies to meet at frequent intervals. All sorts of tuition are provided, there are rallies, shows, competitions and the opportunity to practise and study towards the awarding of test certificates.

One of the things taught by the clubs is the care of your tack. TACK or TACKLE is the term used to describe all the basic equipment used in riding the pony and includes the saddle, bridle and various other items. A Pony Club-approved, general purpose saddle is ideal for use on your pony. It is well made of good quality leather and the vital parts are manufactured to high safety standards. A saddle is an expensive item and it should be possible to buy one secondhand if you wish. It is a mistake to try to save money on tack, however, for good quality leatherwork is expensive and tack-making is a highly skilled profession, so it follows that you will get just what you pay for.

First lessons in riding may be given on the leading rein until the rider gains confidence.

Tack is expensive and must always be properly cared for. Saddles and bridles should be cleaned and carefully stored after use.

Your life may depend on the condition of your tack, for weak leather may break under stress; for example your pony could panic in an emergency situation, and if the bridle or girth snaps at that time you could have a bad fall.

You should ask a knowledgeable person to help you select your tack. A BRIDLE consists of various leather straps and a BIT which goes in the pony's mouth. From the rings of the bit, long leather straps called REINS enable the rider to control the pony's head. Again expert advice is needed to select the correct size and type of bit for your pony, and to ensure that all parts of the bridle are of the right length. Bridles are usually advertised as being Pony, Cob or Horse size, but it is sometimes necessary to buy two bridles of identical leather, but of different sizes, in order to make up one which really fits well.

When fitting the bridle, the cheek pieces should be of the correct length to hold the bit at the right height in the pony's mouth so that it just starts to wrinkle the lips at the corners. The browband goes around the forehead and must fit well, being neither so loose that it droops down or so tight that it causes the headpiece to rub the back of the pony's ears. The throatlatch goes under the chin and, when buckled, you should be able to insert a clenched fist snugly between it and the pony's throat. You should be able to insert two fingers between the nose and the noseband when it is fastened, and the front-band should clear the front parts of the cheekbones.

SADDLES are sold in measurements taken from the front, the *pommel*, to the back, the *cantle*, but vary considerably in design. Reputable saddlers will help you measure your pony and will repad a saddle if necessary to make it fit well. The most important part of the saddle is right up under the flaps where the straps which hold the girth are sewn in, and also important are the bars which hold the stirrup leathers. The hard *tree* on which the saddle is built must be intact, for a saddle with a broken tree is quite useless. When fitting a saddle on your pony, you must make sure that it does not press down on its loins or withers and does not touch the spine at any point. The front of the panels must clear the pony's shoulders and the front arch must be wide enough to avoid pinching the withers. The saddle is held in place by a strong GIRTH which buckles onto straps under the saddle flaps. Whichever type of girth is chosen must be of the correct length to avoid chafing.

STIRRUP LEATHERS must be chosen with care. They should be soft but strong, of the correct length to allow you to ride comfortably, and capable of being adjusted a few holes either way of your normal riding length. The STIRRUP IRONS must be selected so that your booted feet fit comfortably inside. They must not be so tight that your boots could get trapped, nor so loose that your feet could slip right through the irons.

Tack must be carefully cleaned each time it is used so that it is always soft and supple and safe to use and does not rub sore places on your pony's skin. The saddle and bridle are taken to pieces and each section is lightly washed with warm water to remove any mud, grease or sweat. Special saddle soap is then applied to all the leather surfaces and rubbed well in with a damp sponge. All the metal parts are then cleaned and polished, and when the soaped leather has dried it is buffed up with a soft dry cloth before being re-assembled. You can learn the correct method of saddling and bridling your pony, as well as tack-cleaning, by attending club tutorials or helping at a riding school. Always take great care of your tack and never place your saddle on the ground where your pony could tread on it and perhaps break the tree. Never tie your pony up by its reins either, for they or part of the headpiece of the bridle could snap if the animal pulls away in fright. Do not leave the bridle hanging where the pony can nibble at and weaken the leather, and try to avoid letting your pony graze while the bit is in its mouth.

For comfort when riding it is important to have suitable clothes. A protective hard hat is an essential item of equipment whenever you mount up. The best type of hat is made of fibreglass, and has a separately moulded brim which snaps off on impact, saving possible injury to the face during a bad fall. The hat must fit well and may be held in place with a safety harness if required. The second most important item is a pair of stout boots or shoes which enable your feet to take their correct position on the stirrups. Jodhpur boots are specially designed for riding and are safe and comfortable. Whatever footwear is worn, it must have good heels to prevent the foot from slipping through the stirrup iron, and the shoes or boots be able to escape easily from the iron if you suffer a fall. Boots or shoes which stick in the stirrup irons are very dangerous; if you fall off and your foot is caught you will be dragged by your frightened pony and you could receive serious injuries. Rubber riding boots are available and are fairly reasonable in price. They are excellent in wet, muddy weather, being easily cleaned with warm soapy water. When

A beautifully turned-out horse and rider — elegant dress and carefully fitted tack.

Jodhpurs, a jacket and a hard hat are suitable for hunting when it is important to be comfortable and to look neat and tidy.

wearing long riding boots it is a good idea to put an old pair of cut-down tights over your socks for this helps you to get the tight boots off again at the end of your riding session.

Jodhpurs are excellent for riding, being designed and made expressly for that purpose. They prevent the inside of the legs from being bruised and pinched by the stirrup leathers. Costing very little more than good quality jeans, they are smarter, more comfortable and last for years unless unfortunately outgrown. Jeans are perfectly acceptable for use in informal riding, but the inside leg seams can be very uncomfortable, chafing against the legs and offering little protection against the pinching of the stirrup leathers.

For showing or hunting it is important to wear a specially cut jacket, but for casual riding a waterproof and windproof anorak is probably more serviceable. Gloves for riding must be made of finely knitted string yarn; those of any other material slip on the reins and are useless when wet. To complete your riding outfit, wear a plain polo-necked sweater or a neat shirt and tie. Hacking in the countryside is very pleasureable and casual riding clothes complete with hard hat may be worn.

When riding in the countryside it is important to obtain permission before crossing farmers' fields. If you explain that you will always keep to the 'headlands' or perimeters of the fields and will never cross growing crops or scare sheep or cattle, the farmers will generally agree. Assure them that you understand that gates must always be left as they are found, whether open or shut, and that you will never cut up the land by galloping over it during wet weather.

Try to find out where all the bridleways exist in your area. They are always marked on the official Ordnance Survey maps, but may be overgrown, wired up or blocked off in some other way. Do your best to have such pathways opened up by applying to your local authority for help, perhaps getting together with a group of friends to clear away overhanging brambles and patches of nettles which may have obscured the right of way. You may discover some footpaths which are suitable for riding, too, but if you pass hikers, you must give them the right of way, never brushing them or splashing them with mud. Never ride fast along footpaths for you will spoil the surfaces and may also cause accidents. Your inconsiderate behaviour could prevent other riders from being given access to such rides.

Riding on the road is sometimes necessary and you must learn to use the correct signals. Your pony must be good in traffic, for some drivers are very inconsiderate and speed past, giving a terrifyingly loud blast on the horn at the same time. Many drivers do have good manners however, slowing down and passing quietly, and you should acknowledge their kindness by raising your hand in a friendly gesture. Always ride with the traffic and keep well to the side of the road. If you are with a group of riders, keep in single file and station the quietest ponies at the front and rear. Ride on verges wherever possible but look out for rainwater gullies which may trap a pony's foot. If

Find the bridleways in your area — they should be clearly signed.

61

you see something hazardous in front and there is traffic approaching from your rear, give a clear signal for it to slow down by extending your arm and waving it slowly up and down. To turn right, extend the right arm, and to turn left, extend the left arm. Hold your arm up with the elbow bent and the palm facing forward to indicate that you want traffic to stop. Never trot round corners where the surfaces are likely to be extra slippery and never go out riding on the roads when they are icy, very wet, or if it is dark or there is any fog. When you have to cross a busy road, wait until all the traffic has cleared in both directions, then cross smartly in a straight line to the other side.

If your pony becomes very frightened, it is best to dismount calmly and lead it into the nearest gateway or drive until it calms down before mounting up again. Never let your pony think that it has the better of you, or it may become habitually disobedient on the roads and need reschooling by an expert rider.

Riding on the beach is great fun and can be very exciting, but it is not generally allowed during the summer months when there are lots of holiday-makers about. If you live quite near to the seashore, check with your local authority to see if you can get permission to ride along the sands. Even outside the holiday season it is advisable to take such rides early in the morning or late in the evening, when there are fewer people about. You must also check the times of the daily tides and take great care that you do not get cut off on an isolated strand. You must never be tempted into using the breakwaters as jumps for they are massively constructed beneath the sand to withstand heavy seas and gale-force winds. The sand or gravel piled against the break-waters may be very soft and spoil your pony's takeoff. If you hit a breakwater at speed you could suffer a fatal accident.

Top: When in doubt as to which is the correct route, check the bridleway direction on an Ordnance Survey Map of the area.

Above: When riding along bridleways, try to keep them open and free from encroaching weeds and brambles.

Right: Before taking part in parades, you must ensure that your pony is absolutely safe in traffic.

Top: A group of riders about to set off for a desert trek in Old Tucson, Arizona.

Above: Mounted games help to build confidence between pony and rider.

Far right: This pony is obviously fascinated by the sea, but his rider is not suitably dressed to allow him a swimming session.

If you ride on the beach with a group of other riders on a calm warm day, you may decide to try swimming your pony. You will need to wear a swim suit, and remove the saddle. Ride straight into the sea, taking a good hold of the mane in one hand, and keeping the pony's head up so that it is not tempted to get down to roll in the wet sand. Do not go out too far and never go alone in case you get into trouble. If the shore shelves steeply, the pony's shoulders will plunge as it starts to swim and the water will come up to your waist. Let the pony have the freedom of its head and neck and let it enjoy the exhilaration of the swim; then turn it very gently to face back to the shore. You might find that your pony is so keyed up by the swim that it wants to gallop out as soon as its feet touch the bottom once more, so keep it in check but moving firmly forward. Once on the dry land again, your pony will probably shake itself free from water, just like a dog, so make sure that you are nowhere near anyone who might object to a thorough soaking. Salt water is excellent for your pony's legs, but on your return home you should wash and dry the hooves before applying oil to prevent any chance of them cracking.

Picnic rides are great fun and are generally organized by a group of friends or by a riding club. You should wear very casual clothes and put your pony's headcollar on over its bridle, tying the loose end of the rope neatly around its neck. Food and drinks are carried in rucksacks or in bags which may be tied to the metal 'D' rings on your saddle. You will obviously choose a fine warm day for your picnic ride, but it is sensible to take along a neatly rolled anorak, also tied to your saddle. Plan your route carefully, trying to make it a circular one and therefore more interesting, with a suitable place for eating lunch. Hack at a steady pace all morning, keeping your pony cool, and on reaching the picnic site, remove your saddle and bridle so that your pony may have a drink and be allowed to graze, before being tied up in the shade while you and your friends eat your own lunch. Gather up all your litter before saddling up again, and enjoy a leisurely afternoon ride home.

Local shows cater for both experienced and novice riders and usually have classes for ponies at all stages of training, and of varying ability. Some classes are judged on appearance, some on performance and some on a combination of the two. There are classes for the BEST RIDER and for the BEST TURNOUT, and FAMILY PONY CLASSES are for the best all-rounder. The HANDY PONY CLASSES test an animal's ingenuity and handiness, and the miscellaneous classes include the FANCY DRESS PARADE. GYMKHANA GAMES are exhilarating to take part in and to watch, and the ponies seem to enjoy the proceedings just as much as everyone else. In the POTATO RACE the rider needs plenty of prior

practice and a good eye, for the race entails taking potatoes one by one from a steward, or from the top of a pole, at one end of the arena, then galloping back to the other end where they must be thrown carefully into a bucket. Four or six potatoes must be collected in this way and the first rider home is the winner. If a potato is dropped or bounces out of the bucket, the rider must dismount, pick it up and try again.

In the EGG AND SPOON RACE the exhibitor has to carry a wooden cookery spoon in one hand with a carefully balanced potato or hard-boiled egg sitting precariously in the bowl. He has to race down the arena and back again without losing the egg, or holding it in place with a crafty thumb. The BENDING RACE needs a well-schooled and very supple pony able to bend at speed and stop promptly. Lines of tall poles are set at regular intervals up the arena and the ponies are started in line to race to the end of the field weaving in and out of the poles, turning tightly around the last one and galloping back in the same fashion to the finish. No poles must be missed, neither must they be knocked down, or the pony and rider are eliminated.

Lots of competitive mounted games use music which is played while the riders circle in the arena. When the music stops they must hasten to the centre to reach a goal, either to grab a pole or put their hat on one, or dismount to sit on a chair or sack, depending on the game. There are fewer goals than there are exhibitors, and those who do not find one are sent out of the ring. Some of the goals or bases are removed at each round until there is only one left in the centre and two or three determined riders left in the race. A combination of skill, judgment and luck is needed to win MUSICAL POLES, HATS, CHAIRS or MATS. One musical game which needs a lot of skill plus a very obedient pony is MUSICAL STATUES. In this the riders circle and when the music stops abruptly they must come to a complete halt and stand quite motionless while stewards inspect them. Any pony that moves a leg is eliminated, and the game proceeds until one worthy winner remains in the ring.

APPLE BOBBING is very funny to watch for the riders gallop from the starting line to a row of buckets each containing very cold water and a large, hard apple. The riders must dismount, hold their ponies' reins in one hand and with the other hands behind their backs, kneel down and attempt to retrieve the apples in their mouths before remounting and galloping to the finish, apples still clenched in their teeth.

JUMPING CLASSES at local shows provide good practice in ringcraft and procedure for the novice rider and pony. Such classes are generally limited by the height of the ponies and have correspondingly high fences. In most competitions, faults are given for fences brought down, refusals and falls, and the competitor with the least faults is the eventual winner. An enjoyable jumping

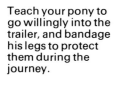

Teach your pony to go willingly into the trailer, and bandage his legs to protect them during the journey.

Right: Clever ponies soon learn how to treat such barriers as banks, usually jumping onto the top, changing legs and leaping off again.

Above: A keen pony jumping confidently and with obvious enjoyment.

Left: Young competitors on tiny ponies are given suitable low jumps.

At two years of age, a pony can gain great experience and confidence by being shown in-hand.

contest is the CHASE-ME-CHARLIE in which all the competitors line up and take turns to follow each other over a few simple jumps. At first the jumps are very low and, if a pony knocks one down or refuses, it is sent from the ring. Each rider is instructed to keep well clear of the pony in front for safety, and the jumps are gradually raised after each has been attempted once. Eventually a few keen ponies and their riders are left in the competition and the jumps might get quite high before the winner is decided.

Truly competitive SHOW JUMPING calls for a skilled rider and a very well-schooled and fit pony. To enter this field you must receive expert advice and tuition and spend a lot of time in building up yourself and your mount to the required standard. For success in this sport you really need to invest in an experienced and proven show-jumping pony, for such an animal will teach you more about jumping than any instructor. The jumping pony is short in the back with a deep girth and short strong loins. The quarters will be very well developed, and the hocks strong and low and said to be 'well let down'. The front and neck will also be well made and such a pony, although it might not be very handsome, will be a free mover and thoroughly enjoy its job.

Jumpers are schooled very carefully at home over quite small obstacles, rarely facing big jumps unless actually in the ring. The schooling sessions are interspersed with hacking during which lots of small natural obstacles may be jumped. The pony is encouraged to trot steadily on such hacks, especially up and down slight hills as this develops the muscles used in jumping.

As well as show-jumping, you could ride in HUNTER TRIALS which have long courses of varied natural jumps of the type you might expect to find during a

Dartmoor ponies being judged in a Mountain and Moorland class.

Wherever ponies are on show, they must be groomed to perfection and be in peak condition.

day's hunting, and such trials give you good practice in taking a variety of fences at a fairly fast pace. It is wise to walk the course on foot in order to familiarize yourself with each fence, and to check the layout of the course. Each jump is marked with a white flag to the left and a red flag to the right so that you know exactly which way you must proceed. Riding in a Hunter Trial gives both you and your pony valuable experience in jumping techniques. EVENTING is also a popular sport and the Pony Club in Britain stages special events for riders under 18, while in America the age limit is 20. Riding Clubs stage one-day and three-day events for riders of all ages.

Ponies may be shown in many other categories, such as the WORKING PONY CLASSES, in which aptitude is judged as well as appearance, conformation and turnout, and the pony is expected to take some low, natural jumps. There are special classes for ponies of various breeds and these may be shown IN-HAND or UNDER SADDLE. Perhaps the most popular showing classes are those for children's riding ponies, which are divided by height limits for the ponies and age limits for their riders. Only ponies of high quality, excellent conformation and impeccable manners stand to win such classes, and they often show evidence of Thoroughbred or Arabian forebears. Registered pure-bred ponies have their own showing classes and are judged against their specific breed standard, so that the most typical specimen present should win, provided that it is also fit and healthy and behaves in the ring.

To show your pony you must school it carefully for the type of class in which it will compete. It must be built up to full fitness and be meticulously groomed with a neat mane and tail and well-cared-for feet. You must study the show rules carefully to be sure that you have suitable tack and clothes for the competition you favour, and to check that your pony is the right height and that you do not violate the rules regarding age. Preparing for a show career entails a careful system of feeding and schooling your pony to be at its peak at the correct time. Methodical grooming must be started several weeks before the show season starts and is continued daily. You must learn to plait your pony's mane and tail unless it competes only in the MOUNTAIN and MOORLAND CLASSES, or is a Palomino when the mane and tail must be allowed to float freely. You must learn to clean your tack to show standard, and to apply tail and leg bandages for protection while travelling.

Knights of old prepare to pack away their trappings and return home after giving an exciting jousting display at a horse show.

An obedient pony is essential and it must be well schooled in the basic paces. An impressive walk is important for this is how the judge will first see you and the pony as you enter the ring. In ridden SHOW PONY CLASSES the ponies are asked to circle at various paces – walking, trotting and cantering – and all should be carried out calmly and sedately and with smooth transitions between. One by one, the stewards indicate which ponies the judge wants to have lined up in the centre of the ring. When you are called, ride in steadily and take your place next to the previous pony in line. Do not get too close, and take the trouble to get your pony standing up square and alert, ready for the judge's individual inspection of it.

The best ponies are asked to give individual displays to show their paces to the judge. If you are asked to do this, walk your pony smartly forward and give a controlled showing. Try an extended trot in a small circle with the pony going forward freely but perfectly controlled, then canter a neat figure of eight, changing legs smoothly at the centre each way. If you have been asked to gallop, go smoothly into this pace from a collected canter and push on as fast as you can along the side of the ring, slowing down smoothly once more to arrive back before the judge, where you should perform a controlled reinback and halt before standing the pony square once more. Such a 'show' performed really well, just as you have practised so many times at home, should go a long way to ensuring that you are in the ribbons. Finally the judge may want to inspect the ponies stripped of the saddles, and then to see them trotted out in-hand. If you are asked to do this, lead your pony away down the arena then, turning its head away from you, push it round and trot briskly in a perfectly straight line back towards the judge. If you are lucky and receive a rosette you must thank the judge with a polite smile, and winners may canter a controlled lap of honour before leaving the ring.

Win or lose, you must never forget that showing of any kind is supposed to be an enjoyable sport, hobby or pastime. If you win, your pony deserves quite as much credit as you, and if you lose, was it your pony's fault or your own? It is not always the owners of expensive winning show ponies that have the most enjoyment, for even the plainest crossbred old pony can make a wonderful companion and give you more enjoyment and pleasure than you would perhaps have believed possible.

Breeding Ponies

Although it is a truly wonderful experience to see your own mare proudly protecting and feeding her foal, there are serious matters which must be taken into consideration before you decide to take up pony breeding. Having adequate accommodation is important, both in terms of stabling and grazing, but providing the correct antenatal care for the mare and post-natal attention to both mare and foal can be very time-consuming. Despite the drawbacks, many successful small pony studs have been established after producing a good foal from a favourite retired mare. In pony breeding, it is more usual to specialize in breeding from pedigree stock as the progeny may be shown in-hand when young and generally finds buyers when up for sale. A stallion must be chosen with care and his conformation should excel in those points where the mare may have some weaknesses. BREED SOCIETIES will often help and advise on suitable mates for mares owned by novice or uncertain breeders, as well as providing information on registrations and other requirements for pedigree pony breeding.

Temperament should also be considered when selecting suitable breeding stock. When visiting your mare's potential mate, you should see that he behaves calmly and in a dignified manner in his box and with his groom. Many stallions nibble and nip at all times, but if they also have their ears pricked up you will know that this is quite natural and affectionate. A stallion with ears laid back, attempting to bite and perhaps also stamping his hind feet, might not be quite so well tempered. If your mare is tractable and kind and she is mated with a similarly tempered stallion, you should have no trouble in the early handling and management of your future foal.

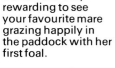

Below: It is very rewarding to see your favourite mare grazing happily in the paddock with her first foal.

Overleaf: Temperament is important in breeding ponies and this little mare is obviously calm and gentle.

From time to time STALLION PARADES are organized by breed societies and these often provide excellent opportunies to see and inspect several potential sires for comparison and at one venue. Some parades cater for single breeds, while others have sections for all types of horses or ponies. When a shortlist of suitable sires has been prepared, you should arrange to visit each stallion at his home, preferably during September or October when they are looking their best and rested after the previous season. It is important to make an appointment to view the stallion and to be punctual.

You will have received a copy of the stallion's pedigree on his stud card or ranch brochure, and will also have details of his fee and conditions of service. There is generally a straight stud fee to be paid, and if the mare proves not to be in foal, a free return mating may be given the following year. Alternatively it is sometimes possible to opt for the 'no foal, no fee' system. In this, no fee is paid if the mare proves not in foal. There are, naturally, quite a few other expenses to be taken into consideration while the mare is at stud: you will have to pay for her board and lodgings, a groom's fee, and any expenses incurred from the veterinary consultant or farrier employed by the stud. While visiting the stallion, all these extras may be discussed and the accommodation and facilities may be inspected. It is sometimes possible to see some of the stallion's progeny, foals perhaps or even some yearlings or two-year-olds.

Once the arrangements have been made for your mare's spring visit to the stallion of your choice, you may spend the winter months in a careful routine designed to keep her in good, hard condition. Her regular worming treatments should be continued under veterinary supervision, and if necessary she should be inoculated against tetanus or receive her booster dose. Some mares show very obvious signs of being in breeding season, 'on heat' – urinating frequently, lifting the tail and showing signs of restlessness and agitation. Your mare should continue to come in season every twenty-one days, so a note should be made in your diary and the stud informed so that a suitable date and time can be made for her to be transported. Most studs insist on a veterinary certificate of health and a negative cervical swab culture certificate before accepting a mare onto their premises. She also needs to have her shoes removed and her feet trimmed before leaving home.

It may be possible for your mare to be taken to stud on the day of her season, satisfactorily served by the stallion and then brought home again. This saves the payment of keep charges, but does not always result in a foal. It is more usual for the mare to be taken to stud just before she is due to come in season, and left to settle down. When ready she will be served and then kept for three weeks before being 'tried'. This entails checking to see whether or not she shows any interest in the stallion. If she does, it means that she is not yet in foal and must be served again. If she shows no sign of being in season, it indicates that she is probably in foal and may return home.

Below: A miniature Shetland foal, just one week old and sheltering from the cool breeze.

Right: The in-foal mare should be encouraged to exercise, but should not be allowed to gallop about.

The mares on wind-swept Lundy Island are allowed to shelter near old buildings during the winter.

When going to stud, the mare should wear a well-fitting headcollar, preferably bearing her name. She may be bandaged if necessary or wear other protective padding if she is likely to be restless or be injured in the box or trailer. Her own snaffle bridle should accompany her, also labelled with her name, for she will wear this during covering so that the groom has more control over her. The actual covering of the mare by the stallion is supervised by the staff of the stud and the mare's owner is not required to be present. Most studs have special yards or areas set aside for covering mares and there is usually a padded gate or barrier over which the two animals are introduced. This is for their protection in case any kicking takes place.

When the mare returns home she should be kept calm and quiet and must not be allowed to gallop about. She may be exercised quietly for the next four months but should not be allowed to get overheated or overtired, or to be subjected to any sharp starts, stops or turns. She should be encouraged to eat good grass right through the autumn and until the winter approaches. IN-FOAL MARES make the best progress when kept in groups with other in-foal, barren or maiden mares, but should be kept well away from any geldings. When the presence of the foal is clearly seen by the increase in the mare's girth, she should be given extra-nourishing small feeds. Hard food such as cubes, oats, bran and maize can be given and fresh clean water must be always available. Most mares greatly appreciate a mineral block which they may lick from time to time.

The foal will be born approximately 340 days after the mare was served and may be delivered in the paddock or in a suitable box. If the happy event is to take place out of doors, it is important that the weather is fine, dry and reasonably warm. The paddock must be well-fenced and level and not have any ditches or ponds into which the newborn foal could fall. It is best to have a loosebox prepared also, in case the weather changes or something goes wrong with the birth. The box must be scrupulously cleaned, scrubbed and allowed to dry right out before laying a deep bed of dry wheat straw banked up round the walls and into the corners. There must be no projections on the walls which could injure either the mare or foal and there should be safe hay racks and holders for buckets of water and feed.

Palomino foals are born pale cream and may not achieve their full golden colouring until their second, third or even fourth summer.

Right: A New Forest Pony foal rests in the spring sunshine.

Most foals are alert and inquisitive, watching everything that goes on, listening and learning.

Mares are very elastic about their due delivery dates and are just as likely to have their foals early as overdue. The first signs of an imminent birth will be noticed at the daily inspection of the mare when the two teats of the now considerably enlarged udder may be seen to be tipped with a waxy substance. This phenomenon known as WAXING-UP usually indicates that the foal will be born within a few days. Another sign is the slackening of the muscles on either side of the spine just above the root of the tail. When labour starts the mare is restless, often kicking or biting at her flanks; she may lie down and get up several times at intervals, and her temperature may rise sharply, accompanied by sweating just before the actual birth.

The FOALING itself is generally very quick and, when the final stage of labour starts, the mare goes down and begins to strain until the foal's tiny forefeet appear in a characteristic 'diving' position quickly followed by its head. Further strenuous effort by the mare pushes the rest of the foal into the world where its first plunges and kicks break the amniotic sac and allow it to breathe for the first time. The mare rests and it is usual to gently drag the foal around to her head so that she may lick and clean it without getting up. The mare still has work to do in order to pass the large placenta, so this resting period is important for her well-being. Once the foal is breathing properly the umbilical cord may be cut unless it has severed naturally during the foal's first uncoordinated movements. The short stump of the cord can allow germs to enter the foal's body, so it should be sprayed with an antiseptic dressing.

After a while the mare will rise and spend a long time nuzzling and cleaning her baby. The placenta should be passed within an hour or so of the birth and must be examined to ensure that it is complete. Soon the foal decides that it is time to organize its legs and attempt to stand up. This can be a stressful time for the owner as the little animal will rise and crash down several times before it sorts itself out and starts to search for its mother's bursting udder. Once the foal has been seen to feed in a satisfactory way and that the mare is not inclined to kick or bite, the bedding may be tidied and the little family left for a much deserved rest. Water and hay should be available if the mare and foal are kept in, and the mare may appreciate a hot bran mash.

Within a few hours of being born the foal must pass its MECONIUM, foetal dung, a waste material present in its bowels before birth. It is a sticky substance, quite unlike normal droppings, and, unless it is passed soon after birth, forms hard balls which block the bowel. Colt foals retain meconium more commonly than fillies, and if there is any doubt about the foal's bowel movement, it is important to seek veterinary attention.

The first milk secreted by the mare is called COLOSTRUM and contains a supply of antibodies to protect the new-born foal against disease. After three days, the constituents of the milk change quite dramatically and the foal can be seen to fill out and grow rapidly. In order to manufacture large quantities of this rich milk, the mare needs feeding well, her grass rations being supplemented whenever necessary. After a few days the foal starts to nibble at its mother's hay, and it will graze in the paddock and taste morsels of the hard feed, too. If the foal is born early in the year, before the first flush of good grass, it may be offered milk pellets which help to give it a good start in life.

Early handling is vital to ensure that the foal grows into a confident and friendly yearling. Foals vary a great deal in temperament. Some are shy and retiring, keeping behind their mothers whenever they are approached; others are confident and inquisitive. It is important to start winning the little animal's confidence soon after birth if possible. Catch up and hold the mare, then extend a hand to be sniffed by the foal. Patience is essential, but you will eventually be able to fondle the little animal's head and neck and fit a well-made FOAL-SLIP of the correct size. This is a tiny headcollar with a little hanging strap under the chin which enables you to easily catch and hold the foal whenever you wish.

The young foal should be caught and handled every day before being fed from a bowl or bucket. Once it allows itself to be handled without jumping or pulling back, a hand should be passed down the neck and over the back a few times. After a few days the foal will allow itself to be patted all over and it must then be taught to have its feet picked up. Leading the mare and foal in and out of the paddock is also good practice. At first the foal is led with one hand on the foal-slip and the other arm held around its rear end to propel it forward in the desired direction while someone else leads the mare quietly forward. After a few days, the foal will allow itself to be led in and out with a rope attached to its foal-slip. Patience and a firm, quiet and gentle manner are essential requisites for the early training of foals, and a little time and effort in these first weeks can save months of work in future years. Later on, the blacksmith may be asked to lift and examine the foal's feet every time he calls, trimming them when necessary and giving the little animal confidence in being handled by strangers.

Overleaf: Care must be taken in protecting the foal. This pasture has many foxgloves on the bank which could be fatal if nibbled.

Below: A heavily in-foal mare trots up for her corn feed, accompanied by her companions.

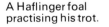

A Haflinger foal practising his trot.

The Miniature Shetland foal is only knee-high, intelligent and very affectionate.

The wearing of a foal-slip or soft nylon headcollar teaches the foal to be handled and helps in catching it each day.

Filly foals are generally more gentle and easier to handle than colts, some of which act just like small stallions, full of confidence and mischief. Such colts must be treated firmly and discouraged from rearing, nipping or pawing with their forelegs before they grow bigger and stronger, when these appealing tricks become dangerous habits.

Your mare will come in season a few days after the birth of her foal and the hormonal changes in her body will affect the milk, causing the foal to have diarrhoea. To prevent the liquid faeces from burning the skin and causing soreness, some petroleum jelly should be rubbed well into the skin of the buttocks below the tail and on the points of the hocks. The mare may be served by the stallion on this 'foal heat', or during the subsequent season, three weeks later, when it is necessary to send her away to stud, accompanied by her foal.

During the hot summer months you may find it wise to bring your mare and foal into a cool dim stable during the day, to rest away from flies and other biting insects. They can be turned out again at dusk to graze peacefully through the night. The foal will be growing rapidly at this stage and should be fed its own rations quite separately from the mare. Eventually the time comes when the foal must be weaned and this is usually carried out when it is about six months old. The ideal way to wean is to find another foal similar to your own and to arrange with its breeder that either the other foal comes to stay with you while your mare goes as a companion to its mother, or vice versa.

The important thing is that the weanling foal is totally separated from its mother and not even within hearing distance, and that both the mare and foal have suitable companions during this stressful time. On the appointed day, the separation is made and should be carried out with the minimum of fuss. The foal must be encouraged to eat well during the following weeks and the mare must be carefully monitored to make sure that her udder gradually reduces in size. She must be carefully confined so that she does not break out of her box or paddock and go off in search of her foal.

After a few days the foal has recovered from the shock of being separated from its dam and should have settled down happily with its companion. Foals need careful management during their first winter, being encouraged to grow a thick coat for warmth and weatherproofing. The mare soon picks up condition once her milk has dried up and she has forgotten about her foal, and if she was covered again shortly after its birth, she will be eager to eat and do well for the developing life beginning to stir again within her womb.